Study Guide for the Praxis *Elementary Education: Curriculum, Instruction, and Assessment Test*

▶ ▶ ▶ ▶ ▶ ▶ ▶ ▶ ▶ ▶ ▶ ▶

A PUBLICATION OF EDUCATIONAL TESTING SERVICE

Table of Contents

Study Guide for the Praxis *Elementary Education: Curriculum, Instruction, and Assessment* Test

► ► ► ► ► ► ► ► ► ► ► ►

TABLE OF CONTENTS

Chapter 1

Introduction to the Praxis *Elementary Education: Curriculum, Instruction, and Assessment* Test and Suggestions for Using this Study Guide

▶   ▶   ▶   ▶   ▶   ▶   ▶   ▶   ▶   ▶   ▶   ▶

Introduction to the Praxis *Elementary Education: Curriculum, Instruction, and Assessment* Tests

This study guide covers the Praxis *Elementary Education: Curriculum, Instruction, and Assessment* (0011) and *Elementary Education: Curriculum, Instruction, and Assessment K–5* (0016) tests. These tests are designed for prospective teachers of students in the elementary grades. Most people who take the tests have completed a bachelor's degree program in elementary/middle school education or have prepared themselves through some alternative certification program.

Test questions cover the breadth of material a new teacher needs to know and assess knowledge of both principles and processes. Some questions assess basic understanding of curriculum planning, instructional design, and assessment of student learning. Many questions pose particular problems that teachers might routinely face in the classroom, and many are based on authentic examples of student work. Although some questions concern general issues, most questions are set in the context of the subject matter most commonly taught in the elementary school: reading/language arts, mathematics, science, social studies, fine arts, and physical education.

In developing assessment material for these tests, ETS (Educational Testing Service) has worked in collaboration with educators, higher education content specialists, and accomplished practicing teachers to keep the test updated and representative of current standards.

The 0011 test consists of 110 multiple-choice questions and covers six major categories of content:

Content Categories	Approximate Number of Questions	Approximate Percentage of Examination
I. Reading and Language Arts Curriculum, Instruction, and Assessment	38	35%
II. Mathematics Curriculum, Instruction, and Assessment	22	20%
III. Science Curriculum, Instruction, and Assessment	11	10%
IV. Social Studies Curriculum, Instruction, and Assessment	11	10%
V. Arts and Physical Education Curriculum, Instruction, and Assessment	11	10%
VI. General Information About Curriculum, Instruction, and Assessment	17	15%

The 0016 test consists of 120 multiple-choice questions and covers six major categories of content:

Content Categories	Approximate Number of Questions	Approximate Percentage of Examination
I. Reading and Language Arts Curriculum, Instruction, and Assessment	42	35%
II. Mathematics Curriculum, Instruction, and Assessment	24	20%
III. Science Curriculum, Instruction, and Assessment	12	10%
IV. Social Studies Curriculum, Instruction, and Assessment	12	10%
V. Arts and Physical Education Curriculum, Instruction, and Assessment	12	10%
VI. General Information About Curriculum, Instruction, and Assessment	18	15%

The tests may be structured in one of two ways:

- The questions will be grouped into the six content areas listed above (e.g., with all mathematics questions together), and in each content area you will answer questions that measure your understanding of curriculum, instruction, and assessment.

OR

- The questions will be grouped into three areas—curriculum, instruction, assessment—with content areas mixed throughout the test (e.g., a question about assessment in mathematics might be followed by a question about assessment in music).

You have two hours to complete the tests. You are not allowed to use a calculator during these tests.

Suggestions for Using This Study Guide

Q. Why should you use this study guide?

This test is different from final exams or other tests you may have taken for other courses because it is comprehensive—that is, it covers material you may have learned in several courses during your entire undergraduate program. The test requires you to synthesize information you have learned from many sources and to understand the subject as a whole.

Therefore, you should review and prepare for the test, not merely practice with the question formats. A thorough review of the material covered on the test will significantly increase your likelihood of success. Moreover, studying for your licensing exam is a great opportunity to reflect on and develop a deeper understanding of pedagogical and administrative knowledge and methods before you begin your educational career. As you prepare to take the test, it may be particularly helpful for you to think about how you would apply the study topics and sample exercises to your own clinical experience obtained during your teacher preparation program. Your student teaching experience will be especially relevant to your thinking about the materials in the study guide.

Q. How should you use this study guide?

As you use this book, set the following tasks for yourself:

- **Become familiar with the test content.** Learn what will be tested, as covered in chapter 3.

- **Assess how well you know the content in each area.** After you learn what topics the test contains, you should assess your knowledge in each area. How well do you know the material? In which areas do you need to learn more before you take the test? It is quite likely that you will need to brush up on most or all of the areas. If you encounter material that feels unfamiliar or difficult, fold down page corners or insert sticky notes to remind yourself to spend extra time reviewing these topics.

- **Read chapter 4 to sharpen your skills in reading and answering multiple-choice questions.** To succeed on questions of this kind, you must focus carefully on the question, avoid reading things into the question, pay attention to details, and sift patiently through the answer choices. Chapter 4 shows you the most common formats that are used for multiple-choice questions.

- **Develop a study plan.** Assess what you need to study and create a realistic plan for studying. You can develop your study plan in any way that works best for you. A "Study Plan" form is included in appendix A at the end of the book as a possible way to structure your planning. Remember that you will need to allow time to find books and other materials, time to read the materials and take notes, and time to apply your learning to the practice questions.

- **Identify study materials.** Most of the material covered by the test is contained in standard textbooks in the field. If you no longer own the texts you used in your undergraduate course work, you may want to borrow some from friends or from a library. Use standard textbooks and other reliable, professionally prepared materials. Don't rely heavily on information provided by friends or from searching the World Wide Web. Neither of these sources is as uniformly reliable as textbooks. Also review other relevant course materials provided by your instructors.

- **Work through your study plan.** You may want to work alone, or you may find it more helpful to work with a group or with a mentor. Work through the topics and questions provided in chapter 3. Rather than memorizing definitions from books, be able to define and discuss the topics in your own words and understand the relationships between diverse topics and concepts. If you are working with a group or mentor, you can also try informal quizzes and questioning techniques.

- **Proceed to the practice questions.** Once you have completed your review, you are ready to benefit from the practice test in chapter 5 of this guide. Then use the following chapter ("Right Answers and Explanations") to mark the questions you answered correctly and the ones you missed. In this chapter, also look over the explanations of the questions you missed and see whether you understand them.

- **Decide whether you need more review.** After you have looked at your results, decide whether there are areas that you need to brush up on before taking the actual test. Go back to your textbooks and reference materials to see whether the topics are covered there. You might also want to go over your questions with a friend or teacher who is familiar with the subjects.

- **Assess your readiness.** Do you feel confident about your level of understanding in each of the subject areas? If not, where do you need more work? If you feel ready, complete the checklist in chapter 7 to double-check that you've thought through the details. If you need more information about registration or the testing situation itself, use the resources in appendix B: "For More Information."

Q. How might you use this book as part of a study group?

People who have a lot of studying to do sometimes find it helpful to form a study group with others who are preparing toward the same goal. Study groups give members opportunities to ask questions and get detailed answers. In a group, some members usually have a better understanding of certain topics, while others in the group may be better at other topics. As members take turns explaining concepts to each other, everyone builds self-confidence. If the group encounters a question that none of the members can answer well, the members can go as a group to a teacher or other expert and get answers efficiently. Because study groups schedule regular meetings, group members study in a more disciplined fashion. They also gain emotional support. The group should be large enough so that various people can contribute various kinds of knowledge, but small enough so that it stays focused. Often, three to six people make a good-sized group.

Here are some ways to use this book as part of a study group:

- **Plan the group's study program.** Parts of the Study Plan Sheet in appendix A can help to structure your group's study program. By filling out the first five columns and sharing the work sheets, everyone will learn more about your group's mix of abilities and about the resources (such as textbooks) that members can share with the group. In the sixth column ("Dates planned for study of content"), you can create an overall schedule for your group's study program.

- **Plan individual group sessions.** At the end of each session, the group should decide what specific topics will be covered at the next meeting and who will present each topic. Use the topic headings and subheadings in chapter 3.

- **Prepare your presentation for the group.** When it's your turn to be presenter, prepare something that's more than a lecture. Write five to ten original questions to pose to the group. Practicing writing actual questions can help you better understand the topics covered on the test as well as the types of questions you will encounter on the test. It will also give other members of the group extra practice at answering questions.

- **Take the practice test together.** The idea of the practice test in chapter 5 is to simulate an actual administration of the test, so scheduling a test session with the group will add to the realism and will also help boost everyone's confidence.

- **Learn from the results of the practice test.** Use chapter 6 to score each other's answer sheets. Then plan one or more study sessions based on the questions that group members got wrong. For example, each group member might be responsible for a question that he or she got wrong and could use it as a model to create an original question to pose to the group, together with an explanation of the correct answer modeled after the explanations in chapter 6.

Whether you decide to study alone or with a group, remember that the best way to prepare is to have an organized plan. The plan should set goals based on specific topics and skills that you need to learn, and it should commit you to a realistic set of deadlines for meeting these goals. Then you need to discipline yourself to stick with your plan and accomplish your goals on schedule.

Chapter 2
Background Information on The Praxis Series™ Assessments

▶   ▶   ▶   ▶   ▶   ▶   ▶   ▶   ▶   ▶   ▶   ▶

What Are The Praxis Series™ Subject Assessments?

The Praxis Series™ Subject Assessments are designed by ETS to assess your knowledge of the area of education in which you plan to work, and they are a part of the licensing procedure in many states. This study guide covers assessments that test your knowledge of the actual content related to your intended specialization. Your state has adopted The Praxis Series tests because it wants to be certain that you have achieved a specified level of mastery of your subject area before it grants you a license to work in a school.

The Praxis Series tests are part of a national testing program, meaning that the tests covered in this study guide are used in more than one state. The advantage of taking Praxis tests is that if you want to practice in another state that uses The Praxis Series tests, that state will recognize your scores. Passing scores are set by states, however, so if you are planning to apply for licensure in another state, you may find that passing scores are different. You can find passing scores for all states that use The Praxis Series tests either online at www.ets.org/praxis/prxstate.html or in the *Understanding Your Praxis Scores* pamphlet, available either in your college's School of Education or by calling (609) 771-7395. You can also find the pamphlet at www.ets.org/praxis/prxstate.html.

What Is Licensure?

Licensure in any area—medicine, law, architecture, accounting, cosmetology—is an assurance to the public that the person holding the license has demonstrated a certain level of competence. The phrase used in licensure is that the person holding the license *will do no harm*. In the case of licensing for educators, a license tells the public that the person holding the license can be trusted to educate children competently and professionally.

Because a license makes such a serious claim about its holder, licensure tests are usually quite demanding. In some fields licensure tests have more than one part and last for more than one day. Candidates for licensure in all fields plan intensive study as part of their professional preparation: some join study groups, while others study alone. But preparing to take a licensure test is, in all cases, a professional activity. Because it assesses your entire body of knowledge or skill for the field you want to enter, preparing for a licensure exam takes planning, discipline, and sustained effort. Studying thoroughly is highly recommended.

Why Does My State Require The Praxis Series Subject Assessments?

Your state chose The Praxis Series Subject Assessments because the tests assess the breadth and depth of content—called the "domain" of the test—that your state wants its education professionals to have before they begin to work. The level of content knowledge, reflected in the passing score, is based on recommendations of panels of professionals and postsecondary educators in each subject area in each state. The state licensing agency and, in some states, the state legislature ratify the passing scores that have been recommended by panels of professionals. (See "What Are the Praxis Series Subject Assessments?" above for where to find your state's passing score.) Not all states use the same test modules, and even when they do, the passing scores can differ from state to state.

What Kinds of Tests Are The Praxis Series Subject Assessments?

Two kinds of tests comprise The Praxis Series Subject Assessments: multiple-choice (for which you select your answer from a list of choices) and constructed-response (for which you write a response of your own). Multiple-choice tests can survey a wider domain because they can ask more questions in a limited period of time. Constructed-response tests have far fewer questions, but the questions require you to demonstrate the depth of your knowledge in the area covered.

What Do the Tests Measure?

The Praxis Series Subject Assessments are tests of content knowledge. They measure your understanding of the subject area that will be your specialization. The multiple-choice tests measure a broad range of knowledge across your content area. The constructed-response tests measure your ability to explain in depth a few essential topics in your subject area. The content-specific pedagogy tests, most of which are constructed-response, measure your understanding of how to teach certain fundamental concepts in your field. The tests do not measure actual teaching ability, however. They measure your knowledge of your subject and (for classroom specializations) your knowledge of how to teach it. The professionals in your field who help us design and write these tests, and the states that require these tests, do so in the belief that knowledge of subject area is the first requirement for licensing. Your ability to perform in an actual school is a skill that is measured in other ways: observation, videotaped teaching, or portfolios are typically used by states to measure this ability. Education combines many complex skills, only some of which can be measured by a single test. The Praxis Series Subject Assessments are designed to measure how thoroughly you understand the material in the subject areas for which you want to be licensed.

How Were These Tests Developed?

ETS began the development of The Praxis Series Subject Assessments with a survey. For each subject, professionals around the country in various educational situations were asked to judge which knowledge and skills a beginning practitioner in that subject needs to possess. Professors in schools of education who prepare professionals were asked the same questions. These responses were ranked in order of importance and sent out to hundreds of professionals for review. All of the responses to these surveys (called "job analysis surveys") were analyzed to summarize the judgments of these professionals. From their consensus, we developed the specifications for the multiple-choice and constructed-response tests. Each subject area had a committee of practitioners and postsecondary educators who wrote these specifications (guidelines). The specifications were reviewed and eventually approved by professionals. From the test specifications, groups of practitioners and professional test developers created test questions.

When your state adopted The Praxis Series Subject Assessments, local panels of practicing professionals and postsecondary educators in each subject area met to examine the tests question by question and evaluate each question for its relevance to beginning professionals in your state. This is called a "validity study." A test is considered "valid" for a job if it measures what people must know and be able to do on that job. For the test to be adopted in your state, professionals in your state must judge that it is valid.

These professionals also performed a "standard-setting study"; that is, they went through the tests question by question and decided, through a rigorous process, how many questions a beginning professional should be able to answer correctly. From this study emerged a recommended passing score. The final passing score was approved by your state's Department of Education.

In other words, throughout the development process, practitioners in the field of education—professionals and postsecondary educators—have determined what the tests would contain. The practitioners in your state determined which tests would be used for licensure in your subject area and helped decide what score would be needed to achieve licensure. This is how professional licensure works in most fields: those who are already licensed oversee the licensing of new practitioners. When you pass The Praxis Series Subject Assessments, you and the practitioners in your state can be assured that you have the knowledge required to begin practicing your profession.

Chapter 3

Elementary Education: Curriculum, Instruction, and Assessment—Study Topics

▶   ▶   ▶   ▶   ▶   ▶   ▶   ▶   ▶   ▶   ▶   ▶

Introduction

The questions on the *Elementary Education: Curriculum, Instruction, and Assessment* test cover curriculum planning, instructional design, and assessment of student learning. There are questions in six content areas: Reading and Language Arts, Mathematics, Science, Social Studies, Arts (including art and music) and Physical Education, and a General Information section that assesses your knowledge of pedagogy (the art and science of teaching). The questions require that you apply knowledge of educational theory and practice to situations that a teacher is likely to encounter in the classroom.

After this introduction, the chapter is divided into six sections that correspond to the six content areas covered on the test. Since the Reading and Language Arts content area covers the largest percentage of questions on the exam, this section of the chapter is the longest and is divided into subsections covering Curriculum, Instruction, and Assessment topics. The remaining five sections cover the material in essentially the same order.

You are likely to find that the topics outlined in this chapter are covered by most introductory textbooks in the field of elementary education, but general survey textbooks may not cover all of the subtopics. You should be able to match up specific topics and subtopics with what you have covered in your courses in curriculum design, instruction, assessment, child development, and so on.

You may also find it helpful to review your state's standards for elementary language arts, mathematics, science, and social studies, which should be available on the Web site of your state's department of education. Another place to look is on the Web site of the education department of a college or university. You should also check to see whether your state has standards for music, art, and physical education. Expect to be tested on the broad goals for teaching all of these subjects at the elementary level.

The "Curriculum" aspect of the test focuses on the organization, materials, and resources of each content area and the implications for using them:

- The broad purposes of teaching all content areas and the purposes of teaching particular topics within each content area (e.g., encouraging self-expression in reading and language arts; developing orderly processes of thought in science; developing awareness of the world in social studies)

- The relationships of subject area "parts" to subject area "wholes" for instructional planning and the instructional implications of these relationships (e.g., the role of phonics in students' whole reading behavior, or how addition is used in multiplication)

- The relationships of concepts both within and across content areas and the instructional implications of these interrelationships (e.g., use of mathematical analysis in social studies; effects of geographical features on human cultures; use of estimation in a variety of problem-solving situations in different disciplines)

- The types and uses of curricular materials, media and technologies, and other resources such as textbooks and trade books in reading; measurement equipment in math; equipment and displays in science; maps and globes in social studies; and technologies like computer software and videotapes

The **"Instruction" aspect of the test** focuses on content-specific teaching and learning principles and their application for appropriate and effective instruction:

- Methods of identifying, assessing, activating, and building on students' prior knowledge, experiences, cultural backgrounds, and skills in each content area

- Methods of preparing, evaluating, and justifying instructional activities within and across content areas

- Teaching and learning strategies to help individual students and groups of students understand topics and concepts within content areas (e.g., demonstration, cooperative learning, guided oral and silent work, use of journals and logs, graphic organizers, and inquiry method)

- Methods for adjusting instruction to meet students' needs (e.g., corrective and developmental instruction, reteaching, follow-up, and enrichment instruction, and preparation of content area instruction to meet the needs of all readers)

- Strategies for motivating and encouraging student success (e.g., praise, wait time, token economies, and time-out)

- Approaches to instruction and the theoretical and empirical bases of these approaches (e.g., developmentally appropriate instruction and model-based classroom management)

The **"Assessment" aspect of the test** focuses on content-specific and general assessment and evaluation procedures and the implications for using these procedures appropriately and effectively in each content area and in general:

- When and how to use traditional and standardized testing methodologies (e.g., standardized tests, basal reader tests, and screening tests)

- Classroom-based, informal, or nontraditional assessment strategies (e.g., observation, oral reports, running records, informal reading inventories, portfolios, and performance samples)

- Interpreting data obtained from various assessment strategies

- Common points of confusion in the content areas (e.g., errors and patterns of error, inaccurate factual knowledge or vocabulary, misconceptions about processes or relationships, and "buggy" algorithms)

Some questions on the test concern general issues:

- The personal, social, and emotional development of children

- Language and communication

- Learning theories (e.g., behaviorism and cognitive views of learning, problem-solving abilities, higher-order thinking skills, metacognition, and constructivism)

- Classroom management (e.g., organization, discipline, procedures, learner responsibility, and interventions)

- Issues of professional growth (e.g., reflective teaching, collaboration, partnerships with colleagues and community, and interactions with parents)

Using the Topic Lists that Follow

The lists of topics will help you prepare appropriately for this test. Try not to be overwhelmed by the volume and scope of content knowledge in this guide. You are not expected to be an expert on all aspects of each topic. However, you should be able to demonstrate your understanding of the fundamental concepts in each topic area. Referring to textbooks, state standards documents, or other sources as needed, make sure you can describe in your own words how each topic is vital to teaching elementary school.

Special Questions Marked with Stars

Interspersed throughout the topic lists are questions that are preceded by stars (★) and outlined in boxes. These questions are intended to help you focus on important, fundamental concepts that are essential for elementary school teachers to know and are critical for success on the test. Some of these questions pose particular problems teachers might face in the classroom, and some are based on authentic examples of student work. Many questions require you to combine several pieces of knowledge and to formulate an integrated understanding. If you spend time on these questions, you will gain increased understanding and facility with the subject matter covered on the test. You might want to discuss the questions and your answers with a teacher or mentor.

Note that the questions marked with stars are open ended, not multiple-choice, and that this study guide does not provide the answers. The questions are intended as *study* questions, not practice questions. Thinking about the answers to an open-ended question should improve your understanding of the fundamental concepts and will probably help you answer a number of related multiple-choice questions on the test. For example, in the section below on Science, under the heading "Assessment," is the following open-ended question:

★ Why is it inappropriate for teachers simply to provide the correct answers for confused students?

If you think about this question, perhaps jotting down some notes on effective ways of teaching science, you will review your knowledge of the subject and you will probably be ready to answer multiple-choice questions similar to the one below:

After conducting an experiment to test a hypothesis they proposed, a pair of students concluded that the hypothesis was incorrect. Assuming that their data are correct, which of the following would be the LEAST appropriate response for their teacher to make to them?

(A) Encouragement, because they have discovered evidence that casts doubt on a plausible hypothesis
(B) A recommendation that they reformulate their hypothesis with the new data in mind
(C) A suggestion that the students repeat the experiment to check their results
(D) An explanation of what the students did wrong

The correct answer is (D). Merely providing an explanation would display a lack of understanding about how science works and would "punish" students for doing good science.

Reading and Language Arts

Curriculum

- ▶ Know what the state and national standards define as the general purposes of students' learning in reading and language arts.

- ▶ Know how to translate curricular standards into classroom instruction.

- ▶ Know how to create balanced reading, writing, speaking, and listening programs.

- ▶ Be able to discern the "wholes" (units) and component "parts" (topics) of a given curriculum.

★ As a beginning teacher, you will probably be asked to teach an existing language arts curriculum. Choose a grade level that you think you want to teach and look over the state standards. Look over a language arts text or curriculum that you might use in that grade. What are its units? How are they broken into parts?

- ▶ Be able to structure learning activities that will enable students to meet larger curricular goals.

★ How might students benefit from field trips, reading aloud, and pictures in the classroom as prereading activities? Think of some other instructional practices that could be used as prereading activities. Identify a benefit for each activity.

- ▶ Know how to integrate language arts concepts within different units of the language arts curriculum and into other subject areas.

★ What are some ways of using reading and language arts to strengthen mathematics instruction?

- ▶ Know how to plan language arts units in appropriate sequences, building students' knowledge and skills from unit to unit and from year to year.

- ▶ Know how to develop age- and grade-appropriate learner objectives in reading and language arts.

- ▶ Know how to choose curricular materials that are developmentally appropriate.

  - ■ Basal readers and anthologies
  - ■ Children's literature
    - — Genres of fiction (novel, short story, fairy tale, etc.)
    - — Poetry
    - — Genres of nonfiction (biography, news article, etc.)
  - ■ Technology
    - — Computer
    - — Video
    - — Audio

★ What are "big books" and what is their purpose?

★ Newspapers can be excellent teaching tools. Can you identify some ways in which you might use newspapers in the classroom?

★ What type of curricular materials, media, and technology might be most appropriate for visual learners? Auditory learners? Sensory learners? Kinesthetic learners?

Instruction

- ▶ Know how to identify, assess, activate, and build on students' prior knowledge, experiences, cultural backgrounds, and skills in language arts.

★ Think of a unit that you might be starting in a language arts class (introducing a book, for example, or beginning to write creatively). What are three ways in which you could determine your students' prior knowledge, experiences, and skills before beginning the unit?

- ▶ Understand how to teach reading.

  - ■ Determining individual reading levels

  - ■ Appropriate planning and instructional techniques to enhance students' literacy growth

  - ■ Facilitating language acquisition and reading readiness

    — Letter-sound correlations

    — Concepts about print (e.g., left-to-right, top-to-bottom, spacing of words in reading and writing)

  - ■ Pre-reading

    — K-W-L chart (What we *know*, What we *want* to know, and What we have *learned*)

    — Word recognition

    — Structural analysis

    — Semantics

    — Syntax

    — Phonics

    — Scanning

  - ■ During reading

    — Vocabulary development

    — Comprehension

    — Control

— Reading aloud

— Word recognition

— Syllabification

— Decoding

— Graphic organizers

- ■ Post-reading

  — Concept vocabulary

  — Writing/journaling

  — Reactions

  — Comprehension and interpretations

  — Rewriting information

★ What are synonyms? Antonyms? Homophones? Why is it important for a language arts teacher to know these terms?

★ What is "phonics"?

★ What is "phonemic awareness"?

★ What is "decoding"?

★ What activities might help students identify main ideas in nonfiction prose?

- ▶ Understand how to teach writing, spelling, and listening.

  - ■ Writing process

    — Prewriting

      □ Brainstorming

      □ Clustering

      □ Outlining

      □ Webbing

    — Drafting (using knowledge of audience)

— Revising

    □ Praise-Question-Polish

    □ Restructuring, deleting, and adding information and details

    □ Conferencing

— Editing

    □ Spell checking

    □ Peer or teacher conferencing

— Publishing

    □ Anthologies

    □ Author's chair

■ Stages of development

— Invented spelling

— Use of words with prefixes and suffixes

— Proper punctuation

— Misformed letters, spacing, and control in handwriting

■ Memorization as a learning tool

— Sight words

— High-frequency words

— Relationships between letter patterns and clusters of sounds

— Spelling patterns

★ Early elementary students often have difficulties learning to spell. How might you help students become more competent spellers?

▶ Know how to adjust instruction to meet students' needs.

■ What is appropriate and why

■ Effective implementation, organization, and planning

■ Reteaching, enrichment, and extensions

★ What is the relationship between different kinds of learning styles and teaching strategies?

★ The students in any elementary school classroom have differing sets of skills in reading and language arts. There will be readers at grade level, for example, along with readers below and above grade level. If you were teaching, how would you facilitate learning for students at different stages of reading development?

★ If you had a first-grade class with children spelling at grade level, and children below and above grade level, how would you structure your class's spelling program to best meet the needs of all learners?

★ What is the difference between students being "on task" and students being "engaged" in an activity?

▶ Know how to use various strategies for motivating students and encouraging success.

■ Feedback and follow-ups

■ Cooperative groups

■ Modeling

■ Flexible skill groups

★ How might you motivate students to read? What are some ways of fostering interest in the reading of fiction, in particular?

★ What are some different ways in which oral book reports can be structured to appeal to all students in a class, ensuring that book reports contribute to students' motivation to read? What are some other ways in which students can share with each other about books they have read?

▶ Know and understand the theories behind various approaches to instruction.

★ According to Piaget, what are the characteristics of children who are in the "concrete operational" stage?

★ According to Johnson and Johnson, what factors must be present to ensure the success of cooperative learning?

★ Summarize, in your own words, important philosophies such as Hunter's work on effective teaching and Holdaway and Clay's work on literacy development. What are some classroom applications of their theories?

★ What is "shared reading"? What is "individualized reading"? What is "guided reading"? Identify and explain the theories behind each of these teaching techniques and think of ways in which you might put them into practice.

★ What theorists have made the most difference in your thinking about teaching children?

Assessment

▶ Know how to analyze student work to guide instruction.

- Identifying students' strengths and weaknesses

- Identifying what students are doing correctly

- Recognizing stages of development

- Identifying and addressing students' misconceptions and errors

- Adjusting instruction

- Patterns of error

★ Name three common points of confusion or misconceptions that new readers in first or second grade are likely to encounter.

★ Name three common points of confusion or misconceptions that fourth- or fifth-grade writers are likely to encounter.

★ What are some ways in which you can help students overcome common misunderstandings of grammar, syntax, and spelling?

▶ Know when and how to use traditional and standardized forms of assessments in language arts.

- Standardized tests

- Basal reader assessments

- Frye Readability Index

★ What does "standardized test" mean? Why do states give standardized tests? Which standardized tests does your state require?

★ To whom should the results of standardized tests go? What might the results reveal? How might you use the information provided by standardized tests?

★ Are IQ test scores useful for teachers? Why or why not?

★ What are IEPs? For what purpose are they used?

► Know when and how to use various informal or nontraditional assessment strategies.

- Informal reading inventory
- Miscue analysis
- Cloze procedure
- Running record
- Anecdotal record
- Conferencing
- Retellings
- Portfolios
- Journals

★ How can a teacher help students evaluate their own work fairly and accurately?

► Know how to interpret assessment results.

★ What kinds of data do you get from an in-class, timed writing sample?

★ What kinds of data do you get from a process writing sample?

★ What kinds of data do you get from an hour-long multiple-choice test?

★ How might you use portfolios in assessing student progress in language arts?

Mathematics

Curriculum

► Know the state and national standards for the general purposes of students' learning in mathematics.

► Know how to translate curricular standards into classroom instruction.

► Know how to plan mathematics units in appropriate sequence, building students' knowledge and skills from unit to unit and from year to year.

★ Choose a general purpose and a grade level that interest you and describe the topics you would teach to children at that grade level to contribute to the general purpose of teaching mathematics. What must children already know and be able to do in order to learn these topics? Choose a different grade level and answer the questions again. If you chose an upper-elementary grade, choose a lower one this time, and vice versa.

► Know how to choose curricular materials and technology that are developmentally appropriate.

- Justifications for and appropriate uses of various tools
  - Hand-held calculators
  - Computers
  - Manipulatives

★ Do you know at least one mathematics resource in each of the following categories: videotapes, videodisks or CDs, computer software, and Internet resources? If not, how could you find out what resources exist for a given grade level?

► Know how to develop age- and grade-appropriate learner objectives in mathematics.

Instruction

► Understand how to teach important concepts, systems, and operations.

- Pre-number and number concepts
  - Counting objects
  - Comparing objects
  - Classifying objects
  - Exploring sets
  - Ordering sets
  - Number patterns

- Base-ten numeration
  - Place value
  - Reading and writing numbers
  - Expanded form of numbers
- Addition and subtraction of whole numbers
  - Computational procedures
  - Relationships between addition and subtraction
  - Relationships between addition and multiplication
  - Relationships between subtraction and division
  - Regrouping
  - Modeling the operations
  - Story problems

★ What are some of the activities you might use with students to teach the elements of subtraction? How would you choose the activities and how would you know if they were successful?

★ Imagine that you had a class of second graders who were much stronger in language arts than in mathematics. What kinds of strategies might you use with your class to help them understand addition and subtraction of whole numbers?

- Multiplication and division
  - Modeling the operations
  - Interpretations for the operations
  - Computational procedures
  - Skill development
  - Story problems

★ What is the connection between multiplication and addition?

★ Why is it useful for students to understand rounding?

★ What is the associative property of multiplication?

★ Why does the multiplication algorithm work the way it does?

★ What is mental mathematics?

★ Imagine that you have students who do not understand the concept of dividing with remainders, students who have trouble applying what they know about dividing with remainders to "real-life" word problems, and students who appear to understand division and remainders completely. How might you adjust your instruction to meet the needs of all of your students?

- Number terminology
  - Factors
  - Multiples
  - Primes and composites
  - Remainders
  - Odd and even
- Rational numbers
  - Fraction and decimal equivalence
  - Computation
  - Modeling

★ Imagine that you are beginning to teach your students the concept of fractions. How might you identify and assess your students' prior knowledge and skills?

★ One way to introduce fractions to students is to discuss money. How might you discover whether there are cultural differences among your students in their understanding of money?

- Problem solving
  - Investigating and understanding content
  - Formulating problems from everyday situations
  - Developing strategies applicable to a wide range of problems (e.g., estimation, approximation)
  - Verifying and interpreting results
  - Building students' confidence
  - Identifying and solving problems that are developmentally appropriate
- Geometry
  - Geometric figures and relationships
  - Nonmetric and metric units of measurement
  - Coordinate geometry
  - Informal geometry
- Measurement
  - Length
  - Area
  - Volume
  - Weight
  - Angles
  - Time
  - Temperature
  - Distance

★ If issues of cultural diversity arise in a class, what are some ways in which you can work with those issues throughout a unit on measurement?

★ Name three ways of helping elementary students understand "area" versus "perimeter." On what theories are these approaches based?

- Probability and statistics
  - Data
    - Counting
    - Organizing
    - Representing and interpreting
  - Intuitive concepts of chance

▶ Be able to demonstrate how you will put your knowledge of learning theories and instructional strategies into practice in teaching mathematics.

- Activating prior knowledge
- Constructing knowledge
- Coaching
- Behavioral approach
- Modeling
- Informal reasoning
- Demonstration
- Cooperative learning
- Guided oral and silent work
- Graphic organizers
- Inquiry method

▶ Know how to apply various instructional approaches to classroom management and student motivation.

- Developmentally appropriate instruction
- Model-based classroom management
- Efficient instruction
- Small-group instruction
- Whole-group instruction
- Creating an atmosphere that encourages questions, conjectures, problem solving, and experimentation

★ Many students fear and dislike mathematics. What are some ways of helping children develop interest in mathematics and feel successful?

★ In your own words, briefly define these four instructional approaches: constructivist, coaching, behavioral, and modeling. Which approach would be most effective and appropriate for teaching a unit on sets? Why?

★ What are some of the most common student misconceptions and mistakes that you are likely to find as a teacher of elementary mathematics?

★ Of these, which do you feel you cannot teach well? Where do you need to "brush-up" before you begin teaching?

★ A "buggy algorithm" is a flawed understanding of a process or concept. What specific "buggy algorithms" can you expect to encounter with elementary mathematics students? How can you assess whether your students have these problems?

▶ Know when and how to use various methods of adjusting instruction to meet students' needs.

- What is appropriate and why

- Effective implementation, organization and planning

- Reteaching, enrichment, and extensions

Assessment

▶ Know how to analyze students' work to guide instruction.

- What students are doing correctly

- Concepts that students are developing

- Misconceptions and errors students may be having difficulty with

- Appropriate methods of scoring

- Appropriate methods of remediation and acceleration

- Appropriate use of rubrics

▶ Know when and how to use traditional and standardized forms of assessment in mathematics.

- Uses of standardized tests in elementary mathematics

- Who receives data about the results

- Best uses of formal assessments in elementary mathematics

- How tests are scored

- How scores are reported

- How formal and informal assessments can be used together

★ Imagine that you have a student whose mathematics score falls into the fourth stanine. How would you explain to the parents what this test score means? (Assume that they have no knowledge of testing or the reporting of test scores.)

★ Explain the following terms in your own words: mode, mean, median, and maximum. The most important thing about all of these terms is knowing what they represent—and knowing that when people use data, they usually select one of these representations. For example, if a group of your students scored 46, 46, 46, 78, 80, 90, and 100 (on a test with 100 possible points), which method of reporting scores would make these look the best (besides "maximum")? Which method would make them look the worst? Answer the same questions for this group of student's scores: 0, 10, 22, 25, 45, 88, and 88.

▶ Know when and how to use various informal or nontraditional assessment strategies.

- Observation

- Portfolios

- Performance samples

Science

Curriculum

▶ Know what the state and national standards define as the general purposes of elementary students' learning in science.

★ The National Standards for Student Learning in Science require that students understand scientific inquiry. Why is this process so important for elementary students to learn?

▶ Know how to translate curricular standards into classroom instruction.

★ Why is it important for students to make tables and graphs as a science activity?

▶ Know how to plan science units in appropriate sequence, building students' knowledge and skills from unit to unit and from year to year.

★ Think of a unit you might be called upon to teach in science (e.g., a second-grade unit on ecological systems or on trash management) and describe what that unit would cover. What prior knowledge and skills must students have to learn this unit? How would you find out whether or not the students have the necessary knowledge and skills to begin the new unit?

★ Design a variety of instructional activities that might be appropriate for teaching genetics to lower-elementary students. Could your activities take place simultaneously, with individual students or groups of students doing different things? Would your activities suit the range of learning styles common among lower-elementary students? What methods would be appropriate follow-up to the activities you developed?

Instruction

▶ Understand how to teach elementary students the unifying concepts and processes in science.

- Traditional scientific disciplines and how they interconnect

- Systems, order, and organization

- Evidence, models, and explanation

- Change, constancy, and measurement

- Evolution and equilibrium

- Conservation

- Form and function

▶ Understand how to teach elementary students how to approach science as inquiry.

- Using appropriate questioning techniques; developing testable questions and hypotheses

- Planning and conducting simple investigations; using controlled and experimental variables

- Gathering data with the tools of science; choosing the appropriate tools

- Organizing and using data to construct reasonable explanations; displaying data; analyzing data

- Communicating investigations and explanations

★ What are some ways of teaching the inquiry method to elementary students?

▶ Know how to choose curricular materials and technology that are developmentally appropriate.

- Books

- Software

- Equipment
  — Rulers
  — Balances
  — Thermometers

- Displays

▶ Know how to teach model building and forecasting.

- Physical models

- Computer simulations

- Deciding what to include and exclude in the model

★ Students are often confused as to the differences between "proportion" and "percent." What materials and activities might you use to teach sixth-grade students these concepts?

★ What do you know about available software and Internet resources for teaching science at a grade level that interests you? If you do not know what resources are available, how would you find out?

★ What materials might you use to introduce second graders to a unit on weather?

▶ Be able to demonstrate how you will put your knowledge of learning theories and instructional strategies into practice in teaching science.

- Learning cycle

- Constructivism

- Discovery learning (inquiry method)

- Coaching

- Behavioral approach

- Modeling

- Informal reasoning

- Demonstration

- Cooperative learning

- Guided oral and silent work

- Journals and logs

- Graphic organizers

★ When is demonstration useful for science instruction?

★ When is cooperative learning useful for science instruction?

★ What are some ways in which journals can help students learn science?

★ What is the "inquiry method" as it relates to science?

★ Suppose you wanted to introduce lower-elementary students to the inquiry method. What activities might you employ? What activities might you employ with upper-elementary students?

★ What are the differences between "think-pair-share" and the "jigsaw method"? Is one better than the other for accomplishing specific goals? If so, which goals are likely to be met by each method?

★ What would you do if your students did not seem to understand the point of an experiment they had just conducted? For example, you have completed an experiment on plants' absorption of colored light, but your students do not seem to "get it." What would you do?

★ Many students are easily discouraged in learning about science. Some have heard that science is really important and have inferred that it is complex and difficult. Others have trouble learning to "think scientifically." What kinds of things might you do as a teacher to encourage the success of your students who are studying science?

★ What is the purpose of offering tokens and stickers as rewards?

★ What is one way of *intrinsically* motivating students to understand the health consequences of smoking cigarettes? What is the danger of using only *extrinsic* motivation with students?

▶ Know when and how to adjust instruction to meet students' needs.

  ■ What is appropriate and why

  ■ Effective implementation, organization, and planning

  ■ Reteaching, enrichment, and extensions

★ Which theorist is associated with the term "visual learner"? What other types of learners does this theorist identify? Describe some activities that might help other types of learners best learn key concepts about the human skeletal system.

▶ Know how to apply various instructional approaches to classroom management and student motivation.

  ■ Developmentally appropriate instruction

  ■ Model-based classroom management

  ■ Efficient instruction

  ■ Small-group instruction

  ■ Whole-group instruction

  ■ Creating an atmosphere that encourages questions, conjectures, problem solving, and experimentation

Assessment

▶ Know how to analyze students' work to guide instruction.

  ■ What students are doing correctly

- Concepts students are developing

- Students' misconceptions and errors

- Appropriate methods of scoring

- Appropriate methods of remediation and acceleration

- Appropriate use of rubrics

★ Explain how and why a teacher's methods for assessing a student's ability to *do* an experiment might differ from methods of assessing a student's ability to *explain* the results of a science experiment.

★ Research has shown that students' misconceptions about science, unless discovered and corrected, persist into adulthood. What common misconceptions do you know that *early-elementary* learners are likely to have about science concepts and terms? What common misconceptions do you know that *upper-elementary* learners are likely to have?

★ What techniques do you know for uncovering misconceptions in students' understanding? What techniques do you know for reteaching to correct these misconceptions?

★ Why is it inappropriate for teachers simply to provide the correct answers for confused students?

★ When a third-grade class is tested on being able to identify the continents of the world on an outline map, 75 percent of the class fail to identify at least two of the continents correctly. What activities might the teacher design to reteach the continents of the world?

▶ Know when and how to use traditional and standardized forms of assessment in science.

- Uses of standardized tests in elementary science

- Who receives data about the results

- Best uses of formal assessments in elementary science

- How tests are scored

- How scores are reported

- How formal and informal assessments can be used together

★ What kinds of standardized tests are students usually required to take in your state? When are they required to take them? What do the tests assess? If you have not seen samples of the test, how might you see them?

▶ Know when and how to use various informal or nontraditional assessment strategies.

- Observation

- Oral reports

- Running records

- Portfolios

- Performance samples

★ What kinds of information does a teacher receive from a multiple-choice, end-of-unit test created by the publisher of a science textbook? What kinds of information does a teacher receive from a cumulative portfolio of a student's work in science over the course of a semester?

★ How might you conduct a portfolio assessment in science?

★ What are some types of portfolio assessments? What is the purpose of each type?

★ Each type of test—true-or-false, multiple-choice, essay, and small-group performance—has its place in assessing student learning. What are some ways in which you might use each type to assess learning in science? Give examples of each.

▶ Know the basic principles of health education that are important for elementary students to learn and what methods are best for teaching such principles.

- Nutrition
- Exercise and fitness
- Safety and well-being
- Communicable diseases
- Substance abuse
- Common diseases

Social Studies

Curriculum

▶ Know what the state and national standards define as the general purposes of students' learning in social studies.

★ One unit of the ten themes that form the National Social Studies Standards is "Individual Development and Identity." What is the goal behind this theme? Why is this theme important in teaching social studies?

▶ Know how to translate social studies curricular standards into classroom instruction.

★ Choose a grade level that you think you might like to teach. What kinds of topics might you pursue under the general category of "Individual Development and Identity" at that grade level?

★ Look at a commonly used social studies textbook at a grade level you are interested in teaching. Look at how the book divides the text into units and then look at the topics within the units. According to the textbook, what are some content area "wholes" (units)? What might their "parts" (topics) be?

★ If you have an older social studies textbook and a new one, in what ways do their treatments of curriculum differ?

★ Choose a broad topic "whole" that you will be expected to teach in elementary social studies and then break it down into its component parts.

★ Social studies is a particularly rich field for applying skills and knowledge from other curriculum areas. Think about how you might integrate into social studies instruction the other content areas you are required to teach in elementary school: language arts, science, music, and physical education.

▶ Know how to plan social studies units in appropriate sequence, building students' knowledge and skills from unit to unit and from year to year.

▶ Know how to choose curricular materials and technology that are developmentally appropriate.

★ It is important for teachers of social studies to help students become comfortable with interpreting and creating visual displays such as maps, charts, graphs, and tables. Where might you find materials that would help students build skills in this area?

★ Think of a grade level you would like to teach, and then think of some specific resources, such as videotapes, computer software, and Internet resources, that would enhance your teaching of social studies. If you do not know about technological resources that you might use in teaching social studies, how might you find out about them?

▶ Know how to develop age- and grade-appropriate learner objectives in social studies.

Instruction

▶ Understand how to teach important social studies concepts.

- Social organizations and human behavior in society

- Self, family, neighborhoods, and communities

- Citizenship

- Social structures
  — Communication
  — Transportation
  — Industrialization
  — Technology
  — Economics

- History, geography, and government
  — State
  — Regions
  — United States
  — World

★ Cultural differences are a particularly relevant topic for social studies. At the very beginning of the school year, what are some ways in which you can become familiar with, and sensitive to, your students' cultural background?

★ What is the concept of checks and balances in government? What social studies area or unit includes the study of this concept? What other concepts might you be likely to teach at the same time that you teach about checks and balances?

★ What social studies unit would you expect to follow a unit on nineteenth-century and early twentieth-century immigration? Why?

▶ Understand how to teach important social studies skills.

- Map and globe skills

- Organizing data

- Problem solving

- Critical thinking

- Comparing and contrasting

- Model building

- Planning, forecasting, and decision making

★ What are "critical-thinking skills"? In general, how can you structure assignments to enhance critical-thinking skills?

▶ Be able to demonstrate how you will put your knowledge of learning theories and instructional strategies into practice in teaching social studies.

- Activating prior knowledge
- Constructing knowledge
- Metacognition
- Coaching
- Behavioral approach
- Modeling
- Informal reasoning
- Demonstration
- Cooperative learning
- Guided oral and silent work
- Graphic organizers
- Inquiry method

★ What are some approaches to social studies instruction that have been shown to be effective in the early elementary grades? What are some specific examples of classroom instruction based on these approaches?

★ What is "brainstorming"? When is brainstorming most useful? When is brainstorming *least* useful? What are some scenarios in which brainstorming would help a teacher become familiar with students' cultural backgrounds and prior knowledge of an elementary social studies topic.

★ When might you use a demonstration in teaching social studies?

★ When might you use guided oral and silent work?

★ How might journals be useful for students' learning in social studies?

▶ Know how to apply strategies of classroom management and student motivation in various situations.

- Participation
- Inclusion
- Organization
- Fairness
- Expectations

★ What are some reasons that elementary students might not engage with social studies?

★ What are some strategies that you think are effective in engaging students in learning about social studies topics?

▶ Know when and how to use various methods of adjusting instruction to meet students' needs.

- What is appropriate and why
- Effective implementation, organization, and planning

★ Imagine that you are planning to teach a social studies unit on life in the colonial, or pre-Revolutionary, period. Think of a grade level you might teach. Then think about ways of meeting the instructional needs of all learners. How would you teach developmental learners (those who are below grade level in reading skills, for example)? How would you teach learners who are at grade level? How would you teach learners with more background knowledge of this subject than the rest of the class? How would you teach learners whose primary language is not English and whose skills in English are limited?

Assessment

▶ Know how to analyze students' work to guide instruction.

- What students are doing correctly

- Concepts students are developing

- Misconceptions and errors students may be having difficulty with

- Appropriate methods of scoring

- Appropriate methods of remediation and acceleration

★ What are some of the common problems or misconceptions that elementary school students are likely to have in social studies? How can you assess students to uncover common problems?

★ What are some ways of making sure that students understand important terms and concepts in social studies?

▶ Know when and how to use traditional and standardized forms of assessment in social studies.

- Uses of standardized tests in elementary social studies

- Who receives data about the results

- Best uses of formal assessments in elementary social studies

- How tests are scored

- How scores are reported

- How formal and informal assessments can be used together

★ What standardized tests in social studies do elementary students in your state usually take?

★ How can you make standardized testing a useful exercise for your students and for their parents?

▶ Know when and how to use various classroom-based, informal or nontraditional assessment strategies.

- Observation

- Oral reports

- Running records

- Informal reading inventories

- Portfolios

- Performance samples

★ What kinds of behaviors might you observe in a social studies class? What might you assess when observing these behaviors?

★ What kind of "performance samples" might you require in social studies? What would you look for and assess in these performance samples?

★ What kind(s) of portfolios might be useful in social studies classes?

Arts and Physical Education

Curriculum

▶ Know what the state and national standards define as the general purposes of students' learning in the arts and physical education.

▶ Know how to plan and design arts and physical education curricula that are appropriate to students' physical, social, and emotional development.

- Muscle control

- Perspective

- Maturity

- Expectation levels

▶ Know how to choose curricular materials and technology that are developmentally appropriate.

★ What kinds of curricular materials and technologies can a teacher use for teaching art, in addition to materials such as clay, paint, crayons, and so on?

★ What kinds of media and technologies can a teacher use for teaching music, in addition to showing and playing instruments?

★ What kinds of materials, media, and technologies can a teacher use for teaching physical education, in addition to balls, bats, goals, and so on?

▶ Know how to develop age- and grade-appropriate learner objectives in the arts and physical education.

Instruction

▶ Understand how to teach important concepts in music.

  ■ Rhythm

  ■ Melody

  ■ Timbre

▶ Understand how to teach important concepts in art.

  ■ Design

  ■ Technique

  ■ Balance

▶ Know various strategies for encouraging creativity and appreciation in art and music.

  ■ Creating a positive room environment

  ■ Capitalizing on individuality, motivation, and cultural variations

▶ Know how to teach important topics of physical education.

  ■ Locomotor patterns

  ■ Physical fitness

  ■ Body management

  ■ Social discipline

  ■ Game and sport skills

  ■ Healthful lifestyles

★ Imagine that you have been asked to teach soccer, softball (or tee-ball), kickball, and volleyball in elementary school. Think of four skills you would probably be required to teach for each sport. Determine the order in which the skills should be taught.

▶ Know various teaching strategies.

  ■ Motivating children and creating a positive atmosphere

  ■ Instructing and demonstrating

  ■ Providing feedback

  ■ Questioning and problem solving

★ To teach music in elementary school successfully, you will need to know "families" of musical instruments. List some of the families you know and some examples of instruments in each family.

★ How might you teach a lesson on a stringed instrument if you cannot play it yourself?

★ Imagine that just before the school year starts in the fall, the budget for art is eliminated at the school where you are to begin teaching—but the time for teaching art is left in the curriculum. Think of a grade level that you might be teaching. Now imagine how you might teach art without a budget. What are some art concepts you could teach without materials? What instructional techniques would you use in teaching these concepts?

Assessment

▶ Know how to evaluate instructional effectiveness and student achievement.

- What students are doing correctly

- How students are progressing

- Misconceptions or errors students may be having problems with

- Assessing student work products

General Information About Curriculum, Instruction, and Assessment

Foundations of education

▶ Child development

- Personal

- Social

- Emotional

- Language acquisition

- Communication skills

▶ Developmentally appropriate instruction

- Stages of physical development

  — Gross and fine motor development

  — Brain development

  — Implications for learning

- Cognitive development

  — Important theorists (Piaget, etc.)

  — Methods students use to solve problems at various stages of cognitive development

- Social and emotional development

- Language development

- Factors that influence physical, cognitive, and emotional development in the child's home and community life

★ As a teacher, how might you get to know your students? What would you like to know about your students? What resources might be available to use for this purpose, including school documents (like student records), documents produced by students (like reports on their families), and other kinds of documents? How could you use such information to help you plan instruction? How might you and your fellow teachers serve as resources for each other in getting to know students?

★ In what ways might you learn from your students?

★ How would you adjust your instruction to meet the needs of students with low motivation? With attention deficit disorder? With limited English proficiency? With gifted skills above the grade level?

★ What would a student with "high kinesthetic intelligence" and "low interpersonal and linguistic intelligences" be like? What would such a student's strengths and weaknesses be in learning new material?

★ Name two common misconceptions or misunderstandings you know that elementary students often have. What methods of adjusting teaching might help students overcome their misconceptions and comprehend more fully?

▶ Theories of learning

- Behaviorist and cognitive views of learning

- Problem-solving abilities

- Higher-order thinking skills

- Metacognition

- Constructivism

★ What aspect of childhood development most interested Piaget?

★ What are the implications of Piaget's findings for your curriculum planning for the grade level you would like to teach?

Curriculum

▶ Curriculum components

- Scope and sequence
- Curricular materials
- Learner objectives

★ Why do we, as citizens, send our children to elementary school? What skills and knowledge do we, as a society, believe that children should develop in the elementary years?

★ What are some of the factors a teacher must consider when planning an integrated curriculum for the school year at any grade level?

★ Imagine that you get a job as a first-grade teacher. What are some of the key concepts that first graders should be taught? Name at least one activity you would do with students to teach each concept.

★ What are "curricular materials"?

★ In general, what materials are available in multimedia and electronic forms?

★ What is a "concept map"? How is a concept map related to "curricular material"? In addition to concept maps, what other innovative resources might you use in implementing a curriculum?

▶ Integration of concepts across the curriculum

★ Name some concepts that carry across content areas at a grade level that interests you. For example, for upper-elementary school, the concept of "proportion" emerges in mathematics, science, and art.

★ Traditionally, the contributions of women and many other groups have been neglected or underemphasized in elementary school curriculums. What other groups' accomplishments should be included in a curriculum? If you do not know how to incorporate the contributions of these groups, how might you find the information you need?

Instruction

▶ General principles of instruction

- Learner motivation
- Learning environments
- Diversity
- Enrichments and reteachings
- Procedural skills
- Planning
- Conferencing

★ What constitutes a valid justification for an instructional activity?

★ What factors determine the strategies that a teacher chooses for teaching a particular topic? Which of these are "student based"? Which of these are "teacher based"?

★ In what situations do you think that token economies might be effective motivators?

★ How does the use of praise change depending on the grade level and age of students?

★ What are some ways to help students accept diversity among their classmates?

★ Many parents and some educators are critical of cooperative learning because there are so many ways for it to be done badly, which often negates its possible positive outcomes. What are the responsibilities of the teacher in creating positive learning outcomes from a cooperative learning task?

► Classroom management

  ▪ Organization

  ▪ Discipline

  ▪ Procedures

  ▪ Learner responsibility

  ▪ Interventions

Assessment

► Evaluating instructional effectiveness and student progress

  ▪ Using classroom assessments to increase learning and motivation

  ▪ Authentic and traditional assessments

  ▪ Analyzing results

  ▪ Effective assessment practices

  ▪ Basic concepts of measurement

★ What are the strengths and weaknesses of the following assessment techniques: observation, oral reports, running records, informal reading inventories, portfolios, and performance samples?

★ Give a brief description of each of the following: working portfolio, showcase portfolio, record-keeping portfolio, teacher portfolio.

★ If you collected your students' working portfolios at the end of the first semester, what process would you use for evaluating them? What feedback might you give to students in your evaluations? What would be some benefits of students' doing self-assessment on their own portfolios?

★ What kinds of general standardized tests do students in your state have to take during elementary school? To whom are these tests reported? If you have not already seen these tests, how might you be able to see them or learn their structure and content?

★ Describe in your own words what "norm-referenced" means.

★ Imagine that you have a fifth-grade class in which all of the students received a score of 50 percent or below on a norm-referenced test. How would you interpret these data? What conclusions might you draw about students' performance on the norm-referenced test? What would you do after reviewing the results of the test? Why?

★ Define in your own words what "criterion-referenced" means.

★ Data interpretation can range from interpreting a standardized score report to evaluating student portfolios. What kinds of data interpretation do you think that you need to learn more about? Where can you find the information you need?

★ What might a teacher learn from studying patterns of errors made by students?

► General issues of professional growth

  ▪ Reflective teaching

  ▪ Collaboration

  ▪ Partnerships with colleagues and community

  ▪ Interactions with parents

Chapter 4

Don't Be Defeated by Multiple-Choice Questions

► ► ► ► ► ► ► ► ► ► ►

Understanding Multiple-Choice Questions

When you read multiple-choice questions on the Praxis *Elementary Education: Curriculum, Instruction, and Assessment* test, you will probably notice that the syntax (word order) is different from the word order you're used to seeing in ordinary material that you read, such as newspapers or textbooks. One of the reasons for this difference is that many test questions contain the phrase "which of the following."

In order to answer a multiple-choice question successfully, you need to consider carefully the context set up by the question and limit your choice of answers to the list given. The purpose of the phrase "which of the following" is to remind you to do this. For example, look at this question:

Which of the following is a flavor made from beans?

(A) Strawberry
(B) Cherry
(C) Vanilla
(D) Mint

You may know that chocolate and coffee are also flavors made from beans, but they are not listed, and the question asks you to select from the list that follows ("which of the following"). So the answer has to be the only bean-derived flavor in the list: vanilla.

Notice that the answer can be substituted for the phrase "which of the following." In the question above, you could insert "vanilla" for "which of the following" and have the sentence "Vanilla is a flavor made from beans." Sometimes it helps to cross out "which of the following" and insert the various choices. You may want to give this technique a try as you answer various multiple-choice questions on the practice test.

Looking carefully at the "which of the following" phrase helps you to focus on what the question is asking you to find and on the answer choices. In the simple example above, all of the answer choices are flavors. Your job is to decide which of the flavors is the one made from beans.

The vanilla bean question is pretty straightforward. But the phrase "which of the following" can also be found in more challenging questions. Look at this question:

Which of the following events would result in a bias that may affect the validity of the standardized test scores for a test that presents multiple-choice questions and uses a gridded answer sheet?

(A) Three students use a geometric pattern to fill out their answer sheets.
(B) A teacher gives the entire class an extra ten minutes to complete the test because three students with learning disabilities need more time.
(C) A teacher selects a test that has questions that match the skills and concepts taught in that classroom.
(D) Students taking the test have taken a different form of the same test the previous year.

The placement of "which of the following" tells you that the list of choices is a list of events that might happen in connection with the administration of a standardized test. What are you supposed to find as an answer? You are supposed to find the choice that would result in bias that may affect the validity of that test.

Educational Testing Service (ETS) question-writers and editors work very hard to word each question as clearly as possible. Sometimes, though, it helps to put the question in your own words. Here, you could paraphrase the question as "Which of these events would threaten the validity of the test?" The correct answer is (B). (Tests cannot be considered valid if the established time limitation used for the standardization is violated.)

You may also find that it helps you to circle or underline each of the critical details of the question in your test book so that you don't miss any of them. It's only by looking at all parts of the question carefully that you will have all of the information you need to answer it. Circle or underline the critical parts of what is being asked in this question.

> An 8 year old tries to ice-skate by moving her legs in the same way that she has done when roller-skating. Which of the following of Piaget's concepts of development does this behavior exemplify?
>
> (A) Accommodation
> (B) Assimilation
> (C) Reversibility
> (D) Egocentrism

Here is one possible way you may have annotated the question:

> An <u>8 year old</u> tries to ice-skate by <u>moving her legs in the same way that she has done</u> when roller-skating. Which of the following of Piaget's concepts of development does this behavior exemplify?
>
> (A) Accommodation
> (B) Assimilation
> (C) Reversibility
> (D) Egocentrism

After spending a minute with the question, you can probably see that you are being asked to choose one of Piaget's concepts of development and apply it to the behavior pattern that is described. The correct answer is B. (Assimilation involves incorporating new ideas and concepts into old ideas.) The important thing is understanding what the question is asking. With enough practice, you should be able to determine what any question is asking. Knowing the answer is, of course, a different matter, but you have to understand a question before you can answer it.

Understanding questions containing "NOT," "LEAST," or "EXCEPT"

The words "NOT," "LEAST," and "EXCEPT" can make comprehension of test questions more difficult. A question containing one of these words asks you to select the choice that *doesn't* fit. You must be very careful with this question type, because it's easy to forget that you're selecting the negative. This question type is used in situations in which there are several good solutions, or ways to approach something, but also a clearly wrong way to do something. These words are always capitalized when they appear in The Praxis Series test questions, but they are easily (and frequently) overlooked.

For the following test question, determine what kind of answer you need and what the details of the question are.

> After conducting an experiment to test a hypothesis they proposed, a pair of students concluded that the hypothesis was incorrect. Assuming that their data are correct, which of the following would be the LEAST appropriate response for their teacher to make to them?
>
> (A) Encouragement, because they have discovered evidence that casts doubt on a plausible hypothesis
> (B) A recommendation that they reformulate their hypothesis with the new data in mind
> (C) A suggestion that the students repeat the experiment to check their results
> (D) An explanation of what the students did wrong

You're looking for the LEAST appropriate response for the teacher to make. (D) is the best answer. Merely providing an explanation would display a lack of understanding about how science works and would "punish" students for doing good science.

 TIP

It's easy to get confused while you're processing the information to answer a question with a LEAST, NOT, or EXCEPT in the question. If you treat the word "LEAST," "NOT," or "EXCEPT" as one of the details you must satisfy, you have a better chance of understanding what the question is asking.

Be Familiar with Multiple-Choice Question Types

You will probably see more than one question format on a multiple-choice test. Here are examples of some of the more common question formats.

Complete the statement

In this type of question, you are given an incomplete statement. You must select the choice that will make the completed statement correct.

> After using the words "tooth" and "teeth" correctly, some children begin saying "tooths" and "teeths." This usage results from
>
> (A) paralanguage
> (B) language production difficulty
> (C) overgeneralization
> (D) poor listening skills

To check your answer, reread the question and add your answer choice at the end. Be sure that your choice best completes the sentence. The correct answer is (C).

Which of the following

This question type is discussed in detail in a previous section. The question contains the details that must be satisfied for a correct answer, and it uses "which of the following" to limit the choices to the four choices shown, as this example demonstrates.

> Jimmy, who is in preschool, is able to take off and put on his coat independently during the school day. However, when his mother picks him up, he expects her to help him get dressed. Which of the following would be the most appropriate teacher comment in this situation?
>
> (A) "May I ask why are you putting Jimmy's coat on for him?"
> (B) "If you put on Jimmy's coat, he will not do it for himself."
> (C) "Jimmy can now put on his coat by himself."
> (D) "It's important that you let Jimmy take care of himself."

The correct answer is (C).

Roman numeral choices

This format is used when there can be more than one correct answer in the list. Consider the following example.

> Which of the following items are appropriate for inclusion in a portfolio that a teacher keeps on each child in a class for assessment purposes?
>
>   I. Dated work samples accompanied by teacher commentary
> II. Anecdotal records and records of systematic observations
> III. Checklists, rating scales, and screening inventories
> IV. Weekly classroom lesson plans and curriculum goals
>
> (A) I and II only
> (B) I, II, and III only
> (C) II and III only
> (D) II, III, and IV only

One useful strategy in this type of question is to assess each possible answer before looking at the answer choices, then evaluate the answer choices. In the question above, "dated work samples accompanied by teacher commentary" are appropriate for inclusion in an assessment portfolio. So are "anecdotal records and records of systematic observations" and "checklists, rating scales, and screening inventories." "Weekly classroom lesson plans and curriculum goals," however, do not belong in an assessment portfolio. Therefore, the correct answer is (B).

Questions containing "NOT," "LEAST," or "EXCEPT"

This question type is discussed at length above. It asks you to select the choice that doesn't fit. You must be very careful with this question type, because it's easy to forget that you're selecting the negative. This question type is used in situations in which there are several good solutions, or ways to approach something, but also a clearly wrong way.

Other formats

New formats are developed from time to time in order to find new ways of assessing knowledge with multiple-choice questions. If you see a format you are not familiar with, read the directions carefully. Then read and approach the question the way you would any other question, asking yourself what you are supposed to be looking for and what details are given in the question that help you find the answer.

Other Useful Facts About the Test

1. **You can answer the questions in any order.** You can go through the questions from beginning to end, as many test takers do, or you can create your own path. Perhaps you will want to answer questions in your strongest area of knowledge first and then move from your strengths to your weaker areas. There is no right or wrong way. Use the approach that works best for you.

2. **There are no trick questions on the test.** You don't have to find any hidden meanings or worry about trick wording. All of the questions on the test ask about subject matter knowledge in a straightforward manner.

3. **Don't worry about answer patterns.** There is one myth that says that answers on multiple-choice tests follow patterns. There is another myth that there will never be more than two questions with the same lettered answer following each other. There is no truth to either of these myths. Select the answer you think is correct, based on your knowledge of the subject.

4. **There is no penalty for guessing.** Your test score for multiple-choice questions is based on the number of correct answers you have. When you don't know the answer to a question, try to eliminate any obviously wrong answers and then guess at the correct one.

5. **It's OK to write in your test booklet.** You can work out problems right on the pages of the booklet, make notes to yourself, mark questions you want to review later, or write anything at all. Your test booklet will be destroyed after you are finished with it, so use it in any way that is helpful to you. But make sure to mark your answers on the answer sheet.

Smart Tips for Taking the Test

1. **Put your answers in the right "bubbles."** It seems obvious, but be sure that you are filling in the answer "bubble" that corresponds to the question you are answering. A significant number of test takers fill in a bubble without checking to see that the number matches the question they are answering.

2. **Skip the questions you find extremely difficult.** There are sure to be some questions that you think are hard. Rather than trying to answer these on your first pass through the test, leave them blank and mark them in your test booklet so that you can come back to them later. Pay attention to the time as you answer the rest of the questions on the test, and try to finish with 10 or 15 minutes remaining so that you can go back over the questions you left blank. Even if you don't know the answer the second time you read the questions, see if you can narrow down the possible answers, and then guess.

3. **Keep track of the time.** Bring a watch to the test, just in case the clock in the test room is difficult for you to see. You will probably have plenty of time to answer all of the questions, but if you find yourself becoming bogged down in one section, you might decide to move on and come back to that section later.

4. **Read all of the possible answers before selecting one**—and then reread the question to be sure the answer you have selected really answers the question being asked. Remember that a question that contains a phrase such as "Which of the following does NOT..." is asking for the one answer that is NOT a correct statement or conclusion.

5. **Check your answers.** If you have extra time left over at the end of the test, look over each question and make sure that you have filled in the "bubble" on the answer sheet as you intended. Many test takers make careless mistakes that they could have corrected if they had checked their answers.

6. **Don't worry about your score when you are taking the test.** No one is expected to answer all of the questions correctly. Your score on this test is *not* analogous to your score on the SAT, the GRE, or other similar-looking (but in fact very different!) tests. It doesn't matter on this test whether you score very high or barely pass. If you meet the minimum passing scores for your state, and you meet the state's other requirements for obtaining a teaching license, you will receive a license. In other words, your actual score doesn't matter, as long as it is above the minimum required score. With your score report you will receive a booklet entitled *Understanding Your Praxis Scores,* which lists the passing scores for your state.

7. **Use your energy to take the test, not to get angry at it.** Getting angry at the test only elevates test anxiety, decreasing the likelihood that you will do your best on the test. Highly qualified educators and test development professionals (all with backgrounds in teaching) worked diligently to make the test the best it could be. Your state had the test painstakingly reviewed before adopting it as a licensure requirement. The best thing to do is concentrate on answering the questions as well as you can. Take the test, do your best, pass it, and get on with your career.

Chapter 5
Practice Test

▶ ▶ ▶ ▶ ▶ ▶ ▶ ▶ ▶ ▶ ▶ ▶

Now that you have studied the content topics and have worked through strategies related to multiple-choice questions, you should take the following practice test. You will probably find it helpful to simulate actual testing conditions, giving yourself about 90 minutes to work on the questions. You can cut out and use the answer sheet provided if you wish.

Keep in mind that the test you take at an actual administration will have different questions, although the proportion of questions in each area and major sub-area will be approximately the same. You should not expect the percentage of questions you answer correctly in these practice questions to be exactly the same as when you take the test at an actual administration, since numerous factors affect a person's performance in any given testing situation.

When you have finished the practice questions, you can score your answers and read the explanations of the best answer choices in chapter 6.

TEST NAME:

Elementary Education: Curriculum,

Instruction, and Assessment (0011 and 0016)

Time—90 Minutes

90 Multiple-choice Questions

(Note: At the official administration of these tests, there will be 110 multiple-choice questions, and you will be allowed 120 minutes to complete the test.)

DO NOT USE INK

Answer Sheet C PAGE 1

THE **PRAXIS** SERIES®
Professional Assessments for Beginning Teachers®

Use only a pencil with soft black lead (No. 2 or HB) to complete this answer sheet.
Be sure to fill in completely the oval that corresponds to the proper letter or number.
Completely erase any errors or stray marks.

1. NAME
Enter your last name and first initial.
Omit spaces, hyphens, apostrophes, etc.

Last Name (first 6 letters) | F I

2.
YOUR NAME: (Print)
Last Name (Family or Surname) | First Name (Given) | M. I.

MAILING ADDRESS: (Print)
P.O. Box or Street Address | Apt. # (If any)

City | State or Province

Country | Zip or Postal Code

TELEPHONE NUMBER: ( ) Home | ( ) Business

SIGNATURE: _____ **TEST DATE:** _____

3. DATE OF BIRTH
Month | Day

Jan. Feb. Mar. April May June July Aug. Sept. Oct. Nov. Dec.

4. SOCIAL SECURITY NUMBER

5. CANDIDATE ID NUMBER

6. TEST CENTER / REPORTING LOCATION
Center Number | Room Number

Center Name

City | State or Province

Country

7. TEST CODE / FORM CODE

8. TEST BOOK SERIAL NUMBER

9. TEST FORM

10. TEST NAME

Educational Testing Service, ETS, the ETS logo, and THE PRAXIS SERIES:PROFESSIONAL
ASSESSMENTS FOR BEGINNING TEACHERS and its logo are registered trademarks of
Educational Testing Service.

(ETS) Educational Testing Service

51055 • 08920 • TF71M500
MH01159   Q2573-06

I.N. 202974

1   2   3   4

CERTIFICATION STATEMENT: (Please write the following statement below. DO NOT PRINT.)
"I hereby agree to the conditions set forth in the *Registration Bulletin* and certify that I am the person whose name and address appear on this answer sheet."

_____

_____

_____

SIGNATURE: _____   DATE: _____ / _____ / _____
                                                                                                            Month   Day   Year

---

BE SURE EACH MARK IS DARK AND COMPLETELY FILLS THE INTENDED SPACE AS ILLUSTRATED HERE: ●

1 Ⓐ Ⓑ Ⓒ Ⓓ	41 Ⓐ Ⓑ Ⓒ Ⓓ	81 Ⓐ Ⓑ Ⓒ Ⓓ	121 Ⓐ Ⓑ Ⓒ Ⓓ
2 Ⓐ Ⓑ Ⓒ Ⓓ	42 Ⓐ Ⓑ Ⓒ Ⓓ	82 Ⓐ Ⓑ Ⓒ Ⓓ	122 Ⓐ Ⓑ Ⓒ Ⓓ
3 Ⓐ Ⓑ Ⓒ Ⓓ	43 Ⓐ Ⓑ Ⓒ Ⓓ	83 Ⓐ Ⓑ Ⓒ Ⓓ	123 Ⓐ Ⓑ Ⓒ Ⓓ
4 Ⓐ Ⓑ Ⓒ Ⓓ	44 Ⓐ Ⓑ Ⓒ Ⓓ	84 Ⓐ Ⓑ Ⓒ Ⓓ	124 Ⓐ Ⓑ Ⓒ Ⓓ
5 Ⓐ Ⓑ Ⓒ Ⓓ	45 Ⓐ Ⓑ Ⓒ Ⓓ	85 Ⓐ Ⓑ Ⓒ Ⓓ	125 Ⓐ Ⓑ Ⓒ Ⓓ
6 Ⓐ Ⓑ Ⓒ Ⓓ	46 Ⓐ Ⓑ Ⓒ Ⓓ	86 Ⓐ Ⓑ Ⓒ Ⓓ	126 Ⓐ Ⓑ Ⓒ Ⓓ
7 Ⓐ Ⓑ Ⓒ Ⓓ	47 Ⓐ Ⓑ Ⓒ Ⓓ	87 Ⓐ Ⓑ Ⓒ Ⓓ	127 Ⓐ Ⓑ Ⓒ Ⓓ
8 Ⓐ Ⓑ Ⓒ Ⓓ	48 Ⓐ Ⓑ Ⓒ Ⓓ	88 Ⓐ Ⓑ Ⓒ Ⓓ	128 Ⓐ Ⓑ Ⓒ Ⓓ
9 Ⓐ Ⓑ Ⓒ Ⓓ	49 Ⓐ Ⓑ Ⓒ Ⓓ	89 Ⓐ Ⓑ Ⓒ Ⓓ	129 Ⓐ Ⓑ Ⓒ Ⓓ
10 Ⓐ Ⓑ Ⓒ Ⓓ	50 Ⓐ Ⓑ Ⓒ Ⓓ	90 Ⓐ Ⓑ Ⓒ Ⓓ	130 Ⓐ Ⓑ Ⓒ Ⓓ
11 Ⓐ Ⓑ Ⓒ Ⓓ	51 Ⓐ Ⓑ Ⓒ Ⓓ	91 Ⓐ Ⓑ Ⓒ Ⓓ	131 Ⓐ Ⓑ Ⓒ Ⓓ
12 Ⓐ Ⓑ Ⓒ Ⓓ	52 Ⓐ Ⓑ Ⓒ Ⓓ	92 Ⓐ Ⓑ Ⓒ Ⓓ	132 Ⓐ Ⓑ Ⓒ Ⓓ
13 Ⓐ Ⓑ Ⓒ Ⓓ	53 Ⓐ Ⓑ Ⓒ Ⓓ	93 Ⓐ Ⓑ Ⓒ Ⓓ	133 Ⓐ Ⓑ Ⓒ Ⓓ
14 Ⓐ Ⓑ Ⓒ Ⓓ	54 Ⓐ Ⓑ Ⓒ Ⓓ	94 Ⓐ Ⓑ Ⓒ Ⓓ	134 Ⓐ Ⓑ Ⓒ Ⓓ
15 Ⓐ Ⓑ Ⓒ Ⓓ	55 Ⓐ Ⓑ Ⓒ Ⓓ	95 Ⓐ Ⓑ Ⓒ Ⓓ	135 Ⓐ Ⓑ Ⓒ Ⓓ
16 Ⓐ Ⓑ Ⓒ Ⓓ	56 Ⓐ Ⓑ Ⓒ Ⓓ	96 Ⓐ Ⓑ Ⓒ Ⓓ	136 Ⓐ Ⓑ Ⓒ Ⓓ
17 Ⓐ Ⓑ Ⓒ Ⓓ	57 Ⓐ Ⓑ Ⓒ Ⓓ	97 Ⓐ Ⓑ Ⓒ Ⓓ	137 Ⓐ Ⓑ Ⓒ Ⓓ
18 Ⓐ Ⓑ Ⓒ Ⓓ	58 Ⓐ Ⓑ Ⓒ Ⓓ	98 Ⓐ Ⓑ Ⓒ Ⓓ	138 Ⓐ Ⓑ Ⓒ Ⓓ
19 Ⓐ Ⓑ Ⓒ Ⓓ	59 Ⓐ Ⓑ Ⓒ Ⓓ	99 Ⓐ Ⓑ Ⓒ Ⓓ	139 Ⓐ Ⓑ Ⓒ Ⓓ
20 Ⓐ Ⓑ Ⓒ Ⓓ	60 Ⓐ Ⓑ Ⓒ Ⓓ	100 Ⓐ Ⓑ Ⓒ Ⓓ	140 Ⓐ Ⓑ Ⓒ Ⓓ
21 Ⓐ Ⓑ Ⓒ Ⓓ	61 Ⓐ Ⓑ Ⓒ Ⓓ	101 Ⓐ Ⓑ Ⓒ Ⓓ	141 Ⓐ Ⓑ Ⓒ Ⓓ
22 Ⓐ Ⓑ Ⓒ Ⓓ	62 Ⓐ Ⓑ Ⓒ Ⓓ	102 Ⓐ Ⓑ Ⓒ Ⓓ	142 Ⓐ Ⓑ Ⓒ Ⓓ
23 Ⓐ Ⓑ Ⓒ Ⓓ	63 Ⓐ Ⓑ Ⓒ Ⓓ	103 Ⓐ Ⓑ Ⓒ Ⓓ	143 Ⓐ Ⓑ Ⓒ Ⓓ
24 Ⓐ Ⓑ Ⓒ Ⓓ	64 Ⓐ Ⓑ Ⓒ Ⓓ	104 Ⓐ Ⓑ Ⓒ Ⓓ	144 Ⓐ Ⓑ Ⓒ Ⓓ
25 Ⓐ Ⓑ Ⓒ Ⓓ	65 Ⓐ Ⓑ Ⓒ Ⓓ	105 Ⓐ Ⓑ Ⓒ Ⓓ	145 Ⓐ Ⓑ Ⓒ Ⓓ
26 Ⓐ Ⓑ Ⓒ Ⓓ	66 Ⓐ Ⓑ Ⓒ Ⓓ	106 Ⓐ Ⓑ Ⓒ Ⓓ	146 Ⓐ Ⓑ Ⓒ Ⓓ
27 Ⓐ Ⓑ Ⓒ Ⓓ	67 Ⓐ Ⓑ Ⓒ Ⓓ	107 Ⓐ Ⓑ Ⓒ Ⓓ	147 Ⓐ Ⓑ Ⓒ Ⓓ
28 Ⓐ Ⓑ Ⓒ Ⓓ	68 Ⓐ Ⓑ Ⓒ Ⓓ	108 Ⓐ Ⓑ Ⓒ Ⓓ	148 Ⓐ Ⓑ Ⓒ Ⓓ
29 Ⓐ Ⓑ Ⓒ Ⓓ	69 Ⓐ Ⓑ Ⓒ Ⓓ	109 Ⓐ Ⓑ Ⓒ Ⓓ	149 Ⓐ Ⓑ Ⓒ Ⓓ
30 Ⓐ Ⓑ Ⓒ Ⓓ	70 Ⓐ Ⓑ Ⓒ Ⓓ	110 Ⓐ Ⓑ Ⓒ Ⓓ	150 Ⓐ Ⓑ Ⓒ Ⓓ
31 Ⓐ Ⓑ Ⓒ Ⓓ	71 Ⓐ Ⓑ Ⓒ Ⓓ	111 Ⓐ Ⓑ Ⓒ Ⓓ	151 Ⓐ Ⓑ Ⓒ Ⓓ
32 Ⓐ Ⓑ Ⓒ Ⓓ	72 Ⓐ Ⓑ Ⓒ Ⓓ	112 Ⓐ Ⓑ Ⓒ Ⓓ	152 Ⓐ Ⓑ Ⓒ Ⓓ
33 Ⓐ Ⓑ Ⓒ Ⓓ	73 Ⓐ Ⓑ Ⓒ Ⓓ	113 Ⓐ Ⓑ Ⓒ Ⓓ	153 Ⓐ Ⓑ Ⓒ Ⓓ
34 Ⓐ Ⓑ Ⓒ Ⓓ	74 Ⓐ Ⓑ Ⓒ Ⓓ	114 Ⓐ Ⓑ Ⓒ Ⓓ	154 Ⓐ Ⓑ Ⓒ Ⓓ
35 Ⓐ Ⓑ Ⓒ Ⓓ	75 Ⓐ Ⓑ Ⓒ Ⓓ	115 Ⓐ Ⓑ Ⓒ Ⓓ	155 Ⓐ Ⓑ Ⓒ Ⓓ
36 Ⓐ Ⓑ Ⓒ Ⓓ	76 Ⓐ Ⓑ Ⓒ Ⓓ	116 Ⓐ Ⓑ Ⓒ Ⓓ	156 Ⓐ Ⓑ Ⓒ Ⓓ
37 Ⓐ Ⓑ Ⓒ Ⓓ	77 Ⓐ Ⓑ Ⓒ Ⓓ	117 Ⓐ Ⓑ Ⓒ Ⓓ	157 Ⓐ Ⓑ Ⓒ Ⓓ
38 Ⓐ Ⓑ Ⓒ Ⓓ	78 Ⓐ Ⓑ Ⓒ Ⓓ	118 Ⓐ Ⓑ Ⓒ Ⓓ	158 Ⓐ Ⓑ Ⓒ Ⓓ
39 Ⓐ Ⓑ Ⓒ Ⓓ	79 Ⓐ Ⓑ Ⓒ Ⓓ	119 Ⓐ Ⓑ Ⓒ Ⓓ	159 Ⓐ Ⓑ Ⓒ Ⓓ
40 Ⓐ Ⓑ Ⓒ Ⓓ	80 Ⓐ Ⓑ Ⓒ Ⓓ	120 Ⓐ Ⓑ Ⓒ Ⓓ	160 Ⓐ Ⓑ Ⓒ Ⓓ

FOR ETS USE ONLY	R1	R2	R3	R4	R5	R6	R7	R8	TR	CS

Elementary Education: Curriculum, Instruction, and Assessment

1. During a unit on folktales, a second-grade teacher wants to help students engage in higher-order thinking skills. After the students read *The Little Red Hen,* the teacher asks the students to justify the Little Red Hen's decision to eat the bread herself. Which of the levels of Bloom's taxonomy does this activity address?

   (A) Application
   (B) Analysis
   (C) Synthesis
   (D) Evaluation

2. As part of a language arts program, a first-grade teacher takes students on field trips, often reads aloud from books, and frequently equips the classroom with pictures and prints. Which of the following student needs is met by all these instructional practices?

   (A) Facilitated social adjustment
   (B) Expanded reading readiness
   (C) Increased motor development
   (D) Improved auditory ability

3. A fourth-grade teacher wants students to find some basic information for a short written report on an American Revolutionary War hero. The students may use encyclopedias, biographical profiles, and the Internet. Which of the following language arts strategies is LEAST likely to be used during this exercise?

   (A) Location of information using alphabetizing skills
   (B) Understanding information using skim-reading skills
   (C) Transcription of information using note-taking skills
   (D) Long-term recall of information using memorization skills

4. At the beginning of the school year, a first-grade teacher observes that a student is unable to use beginning and final consonants correctly while reading. Which of the following is most likely to help the student develop these skills?

   (A) Modeling words in context and teaching decoding skills
   (B) Showing a video of a popular children's story and stopping to discuss words that appear in the story
   (C) Pairing the student with another student who is able to use consonants correctly
   (D) Displaying pictures and corresponding printed words around the room

5. During which of the following stages in the writing process are students most likely to share their writing with the entire class?

   (A) Drafting
   (B) Revising
   (C) Editing
   (D) Publishing

6. At the end of a second-grade reading unit, the teacher reads the following sentences from the response journal of a student in the class:

   > I liked the story. The boy
   > wds a good sun.

   The student needs help with which of the following?

   (A) Synonyms
   (B) Antonyms
   (C) Phonics
   (D) Homophones

7. A class has finished reading a novel. Which of the following actions by the teacher is most likely to foster continued interest in reading fiction?

(A) Calling on students to answer questions about the story's theme and setting
(B) Having small groups of students discuss what they liked and disliked about the story
(C) Telling students that there will be a follow-up assignment to compare the story with other stories they have read
(D) Asking students to prepare a graphic organizer that shows the relationship between story parts

8. A teacher gives students two sets of cards to match. One set contains headlines, and the other contains news articles. Which of the following skills are students most likely to develop as a result of this activity?

(A) Decoding text
(B) Recognizing sight vocabulary
(C) Identifying main ideas
(D) Using context clues to determine the meaning of words

9. A first-grade student wrote, "R dg is bg n blk" and read aloud: "Our dog is big and black." Which of the following instructional activities is most likely to help the student become a more competent speller?

(A) Discussion of the difference between "our" and "are"
(B) Demonstration of left-to-right movement
(C) Explicit instruction in phonics and phonemic awareness
(D) Reviews of the rules of capitalization and punctuation

10. Some teachers require their students to give oral book reports. Which of the following is the best rationale for using oral book reports to motivate students to read?

(A) They provide students with practice in making formal presentations before a group.
(B) They show that students have read the books and know the plots.
(C) They require students to analyze every book they read.
(D) They encourage students to share their reading experiences with others.

11. Which of the following philosophies is exemplified in a classroom where a teacher keeps records of students' oral language and provides opportunities for shared, individualized, and guided reading?

(A) Hunter's work on effective teaching
(B) Piaget's work on child development
(C) Johnson and Johnson's work on cooperative learning
(D) Holdaway and Clay's work on literacy development

12. If a language arts teacher wanted to compare current students with other students from the same state in vocabulary, language mechanics, and reading comprehension, the teacher would consult which of the following?

(A) Standardized test results
(B) Last year's report cards
(C) IQ test scores
(D) IEPs

13. A third grader wrote a self-evaluation as part of the writing portfolio that was assembled at the end of the year.

> I specially like this pice. I worked real hard on making it intresting and showing alot of pixtures with my work. This pice shows me being persistint. Now that I am allmost done with third grade I see me as a real writer. When I first start a new story I feel like I weigh 200 pounds. When I'm allmost done I feel like a soaring bird.
>
> P.S. It has been a great year in 3rd grade!

Which of the following best assesses this student as a third-grade writer?

(A) The student continues to rely heavily on invented spelling rather than standard spelling in his writing.

(B) The student has a very negative attitude toward the writing process and finds it very laborious.

(C) The student's writing skills are adequately developed for the grade level.

(D) The student's organizational skills in thinking and writing are poorly developed.

14. A fourth-grade teacher has students keep all their language arts essays for the marking period in a portfolio. This method of assessment can best help the teacher determine which of the following?

(A) A student's understanding of a specific assignment

(B) A student's probable stanine on a standardized language arts test

(C) A student's general development in writing skills over the time period

(D) A student's ability to turn in writing assignments on time in the future

15. The writing sample below is typical of one student's work.

> Me and my Mom are great buddies. We always go so many fun places together. Just yesterday a friend of ours gave my Mom and I tickets to a terific baseball game.

The teacher can best help this student's writing by reviewing which of the following with the student?

(A) Syntax
(B) Verbs
(C) Pronouns
(D) Spelling

16. The following are tasks that teachers might ask students to perform.

I. Adding 2 + 4
II. Joining 2 blocks and 4 blocks
III. Adding 2 apples + 4 apples, which are shown in a picture
IV. Solving $x + 4 = 6$

In which of the following are the tasks ordered from the most concrete level to the most abstract level?

(A) II, I, III, IV
(B) II, III, I, IV
(C) III, I, II, IV
(D) III, II, IV, I

17. Which of the following problems requires the most advanced understanding of the relationships between arithmetic operations?

(A) $27 + 36 = 30 + 33 = 63$

(B) $\dfrac{7}{8} + \dfrac{9}{10}$ is about 2

(C) $\dfrac{1}{2}$ divided by $\dfrac{2}{3} = \dfrac{1}{2} \times \dfrac{3}{2} = \dfrac{3}{4}$

(D) $105 - 69 = 36$

18. The goal of a particular mathematics curriculum is that students in all grades will use computational strategies fluently and estimate appropriately. Which of the following objectives for students best reflects that goal?

    (A) Students will use calculators for all mathematical tasks.
    (B) Students will be drilled daily on basic number facts.
    (C) Students will know the connections between the basic arithmetic operations.
    (D) Students will evaluate the reasonableness of their answers.

19. Students in a fourth-grade class are learning how to copy line segments and angles from their text onto a piece of paper. Which of the following is LEAST likely to help them?

    (A) Compass
    (B) Protractor
    (C) Straight-edge
    (D) Geo-board

20. A teacher gives students a series of cutout shapes and asks them to determine which contain right angles, acute angles, and obtuse angles. The teacher is most likely

    (A) demonstrating real-life applications in math
    (B) explaining the concept of angle congruence
    (C) using manipulatives to teach place value
    (D) reinforcing geometric definitions

21. A culturally diverse fifth-grade class is ready to begin a unit on measurement. The teacher includes in the lesson plan two questions to ask the class before beginning:

    I.   What units of measurement are used to measure length?
    II. What units of measurement are used to measure weight?

    By beginning the unit with these questions for the class, the teacher is most likely doing which of the following?

    (A) Preparing to teach students how to find perimeters
    (B) Assessing students' prior knowledge
    (C) Evaluating students' understanding of volume
    (D) Alerting students that the unit is particularly important

22. $$\begin{array}{r} 29 \\ \times\ 57 \\ \hline \end{array}$$

Before the students in a fifth-grade class solve the problem above, the teacher has them use mental mathematics to compute 9×7, 20×7, 9×50, and 20×50. For which of the following reasons would it be appropriate to have the students use mental mathematics in this way?

    (A) To show the connection between multiplication and addition
    (B) To prepare for an activity involving rounding to the nearest ten
    (C) To introduce the associative property of multiplication
    (D) To reinforce understanding of a multiplication algorithm

23. At the beginning of a unit on division, a third-grade teacher asks students working in groups to devise their own methods for dividing 156 gum balls equally among 4 people. The teacher is encouraging the use of all of the following EXCEPT

    (A) estimation
    (B) guess and check
    (C) standard algorithms
    (D) cooperative learning

24. When a student does not understand the relationship between decimals and percents after an initial period of instruction, which of the following actions is most appropriate for the teacher to take?

    (A) Assigning homework that will give practice in applying the concept
    (B) Suggesting that the student pay close attention and repeating the explanation more slowly and more clearly
    (C) Reviewing the long-division algorithm with the student and focusing on expressing the remainder as a decimal
    (D) Reteaching the concept using examples and/or manipulatives that are different from those used in the initial instructions

25. A fifth-grade teacher is reviewing percentages with a class. Which of the following strategies would provide effective practice while also motivating students?

    (A) Instructing the students to review the basic concepts of percentages in small heterogeneous groups
    (B) Assigning a homework sheet that includes various types of problems about percentages
    (C) Pretending to be a salesperson in a music store and having the students determining percentage discounts off their favorite CDs
    (D) Rereading out loud the pages in the textbook that cover percentages and working sample problems on the board

26. A first-grade teacher, beginning a unit on sets, gave each table of students a collection of buttons and asked the students to put the buttons into groups. They were not given any instructions about grouping them. When all of the students had finished the task at their tables, each group told the rest of the class what characteristics they chose to arrange the buttons. This approach to instruction is best described as

    (A) constructivist
    (B) coaching
    (C) behavioral
    (D) modeling

27. In presenting standardized achievement test results to a student's parents, a teacher should explain that the student's stanine score of 7 on the mathematics subtest indicates performance that is

    (A) substantially below average
    (B) somewhat below average
    (C) average
    (D) somewhat above average

28. As part of a concrete introduction to basic algebraic equations, students have been learning to use a scale balance to weigh various objects. Which of the following strategies would best help the teacher assess students' skills with this piece of equipment?

    (A) Performance sample
    (B) Written test
    (C) Portfolio
    (D) Small-group observation

29. A mathematics teacher determines that the median score by her students on a test on fractions is 87 percent. The results specifically indicate which of the following?

    (A) The most common score on the test is 87 percent.
    (B) The arithmetic average of the test is 87 percent.
    (C) Half of the students scored below 87 percent, while half scored above 87 percent.
    (D) The highest score obtained by any student is 87 percent.

30.
$$\frac{4}{16} - \frac{1}{8} = \frac{3}{8}$$

$$\frac{5}{9} - \frac{1}{2} = \frac{4}{7}$$

$$\frac{7}{16} - \frac{1}{5} = \frac{6}{11}$$

The examples above are representative of a student's work. If the error pattern indicated in these examples continues, the student's answer to the problem

$$\frac{9}{11} - \frac{1}{7}$$ is most likely to be

(A) $\frac{10}{4}$

(B) $\frac{8}{7}$

(C) $\frac{8}{4}$

(D) $\frac{9}{8}$

31. The table and graph below were produced by a group of students during an activity designed to help them collect and graph data and organize information.

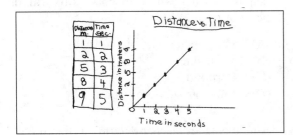

Which feedback from the teacher would best facilitate student understanding?

(A) "You should always use units when measuring variables."
(B) "You should produce a data table to organize your information."
(C) "You should keep the intervals of each axis consistent."
(D) "You should use an appropriate title when producing your graph."

32. The following is an excerpt from a whole scope and sequence for a second-grade science class.

The teacher will open various sealed containers one at a time. Each container will hold one of the following: chocolate, bananas, perfume, soup, oranges, soap, vinegar, and strawberries. The teacher will ask students to raise their hands as soon as they are able to smell the substance. The class will discuss the reason why students closest to the open container usually notice the odor first.

The activity above can best be integrated into which of the following modules from a science textbook?

(A) Life Science: Classifying Living Things
(B) Physical Science: Properties of Matter
(C) Earth Science: Weather and Climate
(D) Environmental Science: Endangered Plant Species

33. Students hung four different cast-iron masses on the spring shown below, recorded the distance that the spring was stretched by each mass, and then recorded the four measurements in the table shown. Next, the teacher asked the students to use the table to determine the distance that the spring would be stretched by a mass of 150 grams.

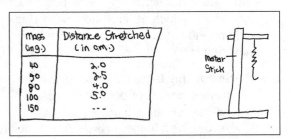

The experiment and the problem posed above would be most appropriate in helping students explore which of the following key concepts of mathematics?

(A) Decimals
(B) Average
(C) Proportion
(D) Percent

34. Literature can be a valuable way to introduce a science unit. A teacher who uses a picture book about clouds in a science unit on weather for second or third graders would most likely use such a book to

    (A) illustrate a process of scientific inquiry for students to use in experiments
    (B) involve the students in using their imaginations in thinking about the sky
    (C) provide a list of facts about clouds for the students to memorize
    (D) present the students with factual information on which they will be tested later

35. Students in a science class have been learning how to separate various mixtures into individual components. Which of the following is the best instructional method to identify a student's acquired skills in this area?

    (A) Have the student separate a few mixtures and solutions while the teacher observes.
    (B) Have the student write an essay about the proper method to separate a few mixtures and solutions.
    (C) Have the student work with a small group whose objective is to separate a few mixtures and solutions.
    (D) Have the student describe for the teacher how to separate a few mixtures and solutions.

36. While learning about plants, students in a particular classroom were engaged in a variety of activities related to the topic:

    - creating a mural
    - writing and acting out a short play
    - observing and recording plant growth
    - composing and performing a song about the development of plants
    - working with the teacher in the reading center, discussing a chapter on plants from the science textbook
    - working alone, reading nonfiction books on plants

    The teacher in the scenario above was most likely providing a variety of activities by which to

    (A) allow a variety of modalities through which students can learn content
    (B) allow students to move around the classroom
    (C) provide opportunities for students to engage in artistic activities
    (D) instruct students in ways of collecting accurate data about plants

37. A science teacher plans to teach a health education unit on nutrition. Students are divided into heterogeneous groups of four members. Each group is assigned a different section of the same article to read, to summarize, and to get ready to teach to fellow students. Students then regroup, with members of each new group drawn from all four of the original groups. Each member of the new group teaches the other three group members about his or her section of the article. This exercise best describes which of the following teaching and learning strategies?

    (A) Demonstration
    (B) Portfolio
    (C) Jigsaw method
    (D) Think-pair-share

38. A class is about to participate in a hands-on science experiment. One student uses a wheelchair and cannot reach the table where the lab has been set up. What would be the most effective action for the teacher to take to ensure full participation for the physically challenged student?

    (A) Give the student a work sheet that covers the same information the rest of the class is learning
    (B) Place the student in a location that makes it easy to observe the experiment from a wheelchair
    (C) Set up an additional lab area in the classroom that is within reach of the student
    (D) Send the student to another classroom until the experiment is completed

39. An elementary teacher offers tokens and stickers as rewards for students who can explain the health consequences of smoking cigarettes. This strategy is an example of

    (A) intrinsic motivation
    (B) extrinsic motivation
    (C) negative reinforcement
    (D) continuous reinforcement

40. Which of the following activities is most likely to help highly visual learners comprehend the key concepts in a chapter on the human skeletal system?

    (A) Taking careful notes when the teacher reviews the chapter
    (B) Rereading the chapter at home with more privacy
    (C) Discussing the key concepts with fellow students in a small group
    (D) Drawing a web diagram of the key concepts presented in the chapter

41. Which of the following processes is used when grouping different types of minerals and rocks?

    (A) Predicting
    (B) Inferring
    (C) Classifying
    (D) Comparing

42. In an upper elementary class, which of the following assessment tools would most effectively determine the ability of each student to explain the differences between mass and volume?

    (A) A true-or-false test
    (B) A multiple-choice test
    (C) An essay test
    (D) A small-group performance test

43. A third-grade class has just completed a science unit on the solar system. After giving the students a blank "map" of the solar system and asking them to fill in the names of the planets in their correct locations, the teacher finds that 86 percent of the class fails to locate the planets correctly. Which of the following teacher responses would be most appropriate?

    (A) Moving on to the next unit because this particular concept is difficult for third-graders
    (B) Moving on to the next unit because this concept will be taught again in fifth grade
    (C) Reteaching the concept with the same methods and instructional materials
    (D) Reteaching the concept with different methods and instructional materials

44. Whenever children are encouraged to investigate scientific concepts for themselves, some inaccuracies or misconceptions may develop. When a teacher's assessment finds that a student is confused, which of the following actions would be LEAST appropriate?

    (A) The teacher asks the student to review the evidence.
    (B) The teacher suggests that the student repeat the investigation, comparing new results with previous results.
    (C) The teacher tells the student to compare results in a small group of other students.
    (D) The teacher provides the correct answer or answers and praises the student for trying.

45. One unit of the ten themes that form the National Social Studies Thematic Standards is "Time, Continuity, and Change." Which of the following questions for an upper elementary class would best address this theme?

    (A) What are the locations of two major oil fields in the United States?
    (B) In what kinds of places has oil been located?
    (C) Why does drilling for oil cost so much?
    (D) Why did the demand for oil increase with the mass production of the automobile?

46. A social studies teacher is planning a unit on the United States Constitution. Which of the following concepts should be taught first in the unit?

    (A) The legislative branch
    (B) The Articles of Confederation
    (C) The Bill of Rights
    (D) The executive branch

47. An upper elementary student selects a pie chart (or circle graph) to show the progression of changes in a town's population over a long period of time. Of the following, which statement is the most accurate assessment of the student's choice of a pie chart for this task?

    (A) The student's choice is appropriate since a pie chart allows the student to display the data compactly.
    (B) The student's choice is appropriate since a pie chart can be divided into as many time periods as needed.
    (C) The student's choice is inappropriate since a pie chart is best used for contrasting and comparing.
    (D) The student's choice is inappropriate since a pie chart requires the use of advanced mathematics.

48. A third-grade teacher developed an activity that requires students to use a mileage chart to plan a trip through Germany. Students were supposed to arrange their routes to include all of the cities listed on the mileage chart with the least possible amount of driving. According to the K-5 scope and sequence of graphic skills pictured below, is the teacher's goal likely or unlikely to be achieved, and why or why not?

Graphic Skills		K	1	2	3	4	5
1	Identifying and Comparing Features in Pictures and Photographs		♦	♦	♦	♦	♦
2	Interpreting Political Cartoons						♦
3	Identifying, Interpreting, and Comparing Lists		♦	♦	♦	♦	♦
4	Interpreting, Completing, and Comparing Tables				♦	♦	♦
5	Interpreting and Comparing Diagrams			♦	♦	♦	♦
6	Interpreting, Comparing, and Making Charts		♦	♦	♦	♦	♦
7	Using and Making Flowcharts			♦	♦	♦	♦
8	Reading a Mileage Chart					♦	♦
9	Reading Schedules and Calendars		♦	♦	♦	♦	♦
10	Interpreting and Making Pictographs		♦	♦	♦	♦	♦
11	Interpreting, Comparing, and Making Bar Graphs			♦	♦	♦	♦
12	Interpreting, Comparing, and Making Line Graphs					♦	♦
13	Interpreting, Comparing, and Making Circle Graphs					♦	♦
14	Identifying and Reading Climographs						
15	Comparing Graphs and Tables				♦	♦	♦

    (A) Likely, because the students have been previously taught all of the graphic skills needed by the time they reach third grade
    (B) Likely, because the students are always receptive to additional fun activities which involve materials other than the text
    (C) Unlikely, because the students would not be familiar with the country of Germany until the fifth grade
    (D) Unlikely, because the students would not be able to use the mileage chart to do the activity because it utilizes a skill that is not introduced until fourth grade

49. A fourth-grade teacher is planning a unit on the history of the state in which the students live. Before beginning the unit, the teacher wants to assess the students' overall general knowledge of state history. Which of the following activities would be most likely to meet this goal?

    (A) Have students brainstorm as a group what they know about the state's history
    (B) Have each student make a list of important events in the state's history
    (C) Have each student choose an event in the state's history and write an essay about why it was important
    (D) Have students interview older people in the community about what life in the state was like long ago

50. A fifth-grade teacher shows students a graph of how the price of home heating oil typically rises during an unusually cold winter. The teacher is demonstrating which of the following economic principles?

    (A) Recession
    (B) Private-property rights
    (C) Supply and demand
    (D) Price controls

51. As part of a social studies unit on Aztec culture, a lower elementary teacher has students make papier-mâché masks that resemble those used by the Aztec peoples in ritual dances. This activity is an example of which of the following?

    (A) Content integration
    (B) Assessing prior knowledge
    (C) Brainstorming
    (D) Using metacognitive skills

52. Which of the following activities is likely to be most helpful for students who are having difficulty understanding the concept of checks and balances?

    (A) Have the students compare the responsibilities of the different branches of the national government with those of their state's government
    (B) Have a group of students make new rules for the class, have another group interpret the rules, and have one student make sure that the rules are carried out
    (C) Have students read their state's constitution and write an essay about some of the state's major problems
    (D) Have students read the section of their textbook dealing with checks and balances, taking notes and looking up all unfamiliar vocabulary words

53. At the end of a unit on nineteenth-century and early twentieth-century immigration to the United States, several students express a desire to explore the ideas of the unit further. Of the following, which is most likely to provide these students with enrichment activities that require their use of critical-thinking skills on this topic?

    (A) Asking them to draw posters about cities that were greatly affected by immigration
    (B) Providing them with photos of newly arrived immigrants at Ellis Island and asking them to write stories that describe these immigrants' lives
    (C) Having them find words in the dictionary that come from other languages
    (D) Assigning them a variety of works of historical fiction from the nineteenth century for independent reading

54. A fifth-grade teacher has been reviewing the main events that led up to the American Revolutionary War from 1750. The teacher has assigned students a timeline to create individually. Which of the following strategies is the most educationally appropriate for motivating all of the students in the class to create accurate timelines?

(A) Placing a colorful sticker on the timelines that are accurate

(B) Allowing the class to act out a short, fun historical play if 90 percent of the students turn in accurate timelines

(C) Telling the students who turn in accurate timelines what a great job they did

(D) Giving the students who turn in accurate timelines an extra five minutes of recess

55.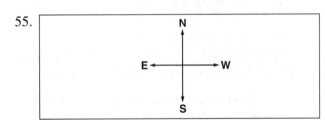

After a geography lesson on cardinal points, nearly one-half of the students in a first-grade class label a compass as shown above. Which of the following is the LEAST developmentally appropriate strategy to help these students?

(A) Place an "E" sticker on the students' right hand and a "W" sticker on their left hand

(B) Have students use hand-held compasses to find their way around the school

(C) Teach students a song that names each direction as they move clockwise around a compass on the floor

(D) Assign students to locate and list ten cities in the Eastern Hemisphere and ten in the Western Hemisphere

56 A third-grade class is learning about the 50 states of the Unites States and their capitals. The teacher uses a variety of independent, whole-class, and at-home learning activities to meet the objectives of the unit. After testing the students on all of the objectives, the teacher compares individual student performance to the performance of the other students in the class.

The evaluation described above is best characterized as which of the following?

I. Formative
II. Summative
III. Norm referenced
IV. Criterion referenced

(A) I and III only
(B) I and IV only
(C) II and III only
(D) II and IV only

57. A student in an upper elementary grade was asked to use a map of the Western Hemisphere to answer questions about places, landmarks, and geographical features. This activity would best assess which of the following social studies skills?

(A) Building models and hypotheses
(B) Interpreting graphic representations
(C) Understanding the lessons of history
(D) Predicting data outcomes

58. A fourth-grade teacher gave an end-of-unit test on the various methods of transportation that existed before the twentieth century. The test consisted of several multiple-choice questions and two essays to be chosen from a range of topics. Most of the students did very well on the multiple-choice questions but poorly on the essays. Which of the following teacher responses would be most appropriate?

(A) Review general essay writing, have students write a few sample essays, assess them, then re-administer a new essay test on transportation

(B) Move on to methods of transportation in the twentieth century, but do not include essays as part of the assessment

(C) Review all the material and give another complete test, with multiple-choice and essay questions

(D) Give grades based only on the multiple-choice questions

59. When students were asked to name three human needs, the teacher received the following responses.

Student A	Student B	Student C	Student D
basketball	doll house	car	food
pizza	parents	video games	clothes
camcorder	dresses	house	air

Which student demonstrates an understanding of human needs versus human wants?

(A) Student A
(B) Student B
(C) Student C
(D) Student D

60. As elementary school students progress in the area of art production, it is LEAST important for them to develop the ability to

(A) use art materials effectively
(B) use multiple processes in artwork
(C) see relationships among their work, their world, and their imaginations
(D) represent figures and objects with a high degree of accuracy

61. A physical education teacher is planning a unit on basketball. Which of the following is this teacher most likely to teach last?

(A) Some simple offensive plays
(B) Dribbling the ball
(C) Passing the ball
(D) How to shoot a layup

62. Which of the following is the best example of an interdisciplinary activity in mathematics and physical education for fourth-grade students?

(A) Conducting a mathematics class outside on a warm spring day
(B) Encouraging all students to keep score during a baseball game
(C) Calculating the ideal trajectory for a basketball free throw
(D) Keeping a record of students' long-jump distances and graphing the results

63. Which of the following is LEAST likely to be included in a unit on stringed instruments?

(A) An audiotape of Spanish guitar music
(B) A videotape of people playing violins
(C) A teacher playing the piano
(D) A teacher playing the banjo

64. The following steps should be used to teach a music concept in a general music class:

    I.   Preparation
    II.   Extension
    III. Practice
    IV. Presentation

Which of the following is the most appropriate sequence for these steps?

(A) I, II, III, IV
(B) III, I, IV, II
(C) I, IV, III, II
(D) IV, II, I, III

65. Aerobic exercise is best described as an activity that requires which of the following to generate energy?

(A) Little or no oxygen
(B) Significant amounts of oxygen
(C) Strength and speed
(D) Flexibility

66. Which of the following is the most appropriate statement to make to students who will be engaging in a brainstorming activity in their art class?

(A) "Say only your very best idea."
(B) "We want original ideas from your own mind."
(C) "Don't judge ideas now; we can do that later."
(D) "Make sure your ideas make sense before saying them."

67. For a music lesson on how sounds are created, a teacher has groups of students create simple musical instruments and demonstrate together how to play them. The form of instruction being used can best be described as

(A) experimentation
(B) cooperative learning
(C) portfolio assessment
(D) lecturing

68. Which of the following teaching and learning strategies would best help highly visual learners remember the major groups of orchestral instruments?

(A) Cooperative learning
(B) Think-pair-share
(C) A graphic organizer
(D) A lecture

69. A teacher would best help a student who always sings off-key by

(A) encouraging the student to sing as softly as possible
(B) praising the student generously
(C) using learning activities such as tone-matching games
(D) assigning music for the student to listen to at home

70. An elementary school music teacher finds that band students love playing upbeat, popular tunes and are not enthusiastic about playing classical music. The teacher hears protests whenever students are asked to play a classical piece. The teacher decides to tell students, "If you do a good job on this piece, one time through, then we will play one song of your choice." This teacher is demonstrating which of the following?

(A) Wait time
(B) Positive reinforcement
(C) Token economies
(D) Time-out

71. According to Piaget, students who are not yet in the concrete operational stage might have trouble in an art class that has group projects because these students have difficulty

(A) performing goal-directed actions
(B) manipulating materials to represent a vision
(C) engaging in a collective dialogue with their peers
(D) understanding that objects can exist whether one sees them or not

72. At the end of a unit, a music teacher wants to determine whether students can explain three major influences on composers of the Romantic period. Which of the following types of tests would be most appropriate to use?

(A) Multiple-choice
(B) Essay
(C) Portfolio
(D) Performance

73. A music teacher has taught several thematic units throughout the marking period. Which of the following is LEAST appropriately assessed by portfolios?

(A) Students' responses to musical selections
(B) Influences on composers students have studied
(C) Comparisons of major musical trends
(D) Knowledge of musical notes on the bass clef

74. An elementary physical education teacher wants to determine whether or not students meet the criteria shown below for an underhand volleyball serve.

I. The server does not step over the line.
II. The server hits the ball with the correct motion.
III. The ball clears the net and goes into fair play.

Which of the following is the best form of evaluation for the teacher to use to determine whether students meet the criteria?

(A) Written test
(B) Portfolio assessment
(C) Teacher observation checklist
(D) Student journal

75. After teaching a unit on symmetry, an elementary art teacher informally assessed the class and found that a significant number of students had difficulty understanding the concept. The teacher then discussed symmetry in new ways, answered students' questions, and asked the students to write a short description of symmetry. The art teacher was doing all of the following EXCEPT

(A) promoting student comprehension
(B) evaluating and refining instruction
(C) teaching for understanding
(D) using standardized testing

76. An elementary school teacher wants students to become lifelong readers. Which of the following is LEAST likely to help achieve that goal?

(A) Giving students a choice of books to read for a book report
(B) Providing students with time each day to read a book of their own choosing
(C) Assigning each student an author about whom they are to read a biography
(D) Reading aloud books that are interesting and exciting, even if some are above grade level

77. The theories of the Swiss psychologist Jean Piaget have implications for all of the following areas of curriculum planning EXCEPT

(A) understanding how children think
(B) using concrete materials in teaching
(C) constructing a rich social environment
(D) sequencing instruction appropriately

78. Of the following, the best way to present the contributions of women of both the past and the present would be to

(A) invite important community resource people to speak on the role of women in the workplace
(B) ask students' parents to become involved in classroom learning
(C) incorporate information about the accomplishments of women into as many subject areas as possible
(D) include a social studies unit on famous women at each grade level

79. A teacher starts a new position in January as a fourth-grade teacher. Many of the students in the class come from homes where English is not the primary language. Which of the following would be the most appropriate way for the teacher to develop good communication with parents and guardians?

    (A)   Have the class newsletter translated into the appropriate languages

    (B)   Visit each student's home to learn more about the family's cultures

    (C)   Invite each student's parents or guardians to visit the school

    (D)   Call each student's home to provide important information

80. All of the following are instructionally sound reasons for using a concept map EXCEPT to

    (A)   assess students' progress in writing a report

    (B)   gauge prior knowledge of a topic

    (C)   serve as a review before a test

    (D)   function as an end-of-lesson, chapter, or unit evaluation

81. All of the following are ways in which an elementary school teacher can accommodate differences in students' backgrounds and help students become successful EXCEPT

    (A)   assessing students' prior knowledge of topics to be taught

    (B)   leading discussions that build on students' common experiences

    (C)   offering students opportunities to write about their family backgrounds

    (D)   focusing classroom discussions on a particular group of minority students

82. A third-grade teacher is planning a social studies unit. The teacher will focus student work on a novel that includes descriptions of nature, Native American culture, and wilderness survival techniques. This type of instruction is an example of which of the following?

    (A)   The diagnostic-prescriptive method

    (B)   Integration through thematic units

    (C)   Team teaching

    (D)   The empirical approach

83. Which of the following is NOT a primary goal of a cooperative-learning approach?

    (A)   Students will be motivated to help one another.

    (B)   Students will develop time-management skills.

    (C)   Students will have a stake in one another's successful learning.

    (D)   Students will be able to explain what they are learning to other students.

84. Early in the school year, a teacher who uses cooperative groups finds that one student in a particular group is too immature to work productively. The teacher could address this problem in the short term by doing which of the following?

    (A)   Limiting the amount of time the class spends in cooperative groups

    (B)   Increasing the number of students in this student's group to offset the lack of contribution from this student

    (C)   Working with this student individually as well as allowing the student to participate in the group

    (D)   Encouraging other students in the group to do this student's share of the work

85. "Wait time" is most useful as a strategy when a student is

    (A)   not focused

    (B)   thinking

    (C)   embarrassed

    (D)   speaking

86. According to Howard Gardner's theory of multiple intelligences, a student with high kinesthetic intelligence and low interpersonal and linguistic intelligence would be most likely to learn science concepts in which of the following ways?

    (A)   Discussing them with other students

    (B)   Finding ways to act them out

    (C)   Writing about them

    (D)   Reading about them

87. Criterion-referenced methods of reporting student achievement are based on

(A) a score that compares each student's score with the scores of other students in the same class

(B) a score that compares each student's score to that of a national group that has taken the same test

(C) the number of questions each student answered correctly for given objectives

(D) each student's standing in terms of grade and month in the school year, in relation to others who took the test

88. Which one of the following types of portfolios is generally considered to present the most accurate picture of a student's progress and development over time?

(A) Working portfolio

(B) Showcase portfolio

(C) Record-keeping portfolio

(D) Teacher portfolio

89. A second-grade teacher determines that all of the students in a class received a score of 50 percent or below on a norm-referenced science test. Which of the following is the best description of the basis of these results?

(A) The students' scores are based on their own degree of success in completing certain prescribed tasks.

(B) The students' scores are based on comparison with standards determined by testing a selected pool of individuals.

(C) The students' scores are based on their performance of a task in real life.

(D) The students' scores are based on anecdotal records kept by the teacher.

90. A small group of second-grade students is reading a story together aloud. Some of the students seem puzzled when they hear the word "sparkled." To make sure that all of the students understand the word, the teacher asks a student to read the rest of the paragraph aloud. Then, when the student has finished reading, the teacher asks the group: "How did the character in the story feel as she spoke, and what did her eyes do to show her excitement?" The teacher is helping students to use which of the following word-comprehension strategies?

(A) Phonic clues

(B) Context clues

(C) Configuration clues

(D) Morphemic clues

Chapter 6
Right Answers and Explanations

▶   ▶   ▶   ▶   ▶   ▶   ▶   ▶   ▶   ▶   ▶   ▶

Right Answers and Content Categories

Now that you have answered all of the practice questions, you can check your work. Compare your answers with the correct answers in the table below.

Question Number	Correct Answer	Content Category	Question Number	Correct Answer	Content Category
1	D	Reading and Language Arts Curriculum	46	B	Social Studies Curriculum
2	B	Reading and Language Arts Curriculum	47	C	Social Studies Curriculum
3	D	Reading and Language Arts Curriculum	48	D	Social Studies Curriculum
4	A	Reading and Language Arts Curriculum	49	A	Social Studies Instruction
5	D	Reading and Language Arts Curriculum	50	C	Social Studies Instruction
6	D	Reading and Language Arts Instruction	51	A	Social Studies Instruction
7	B	Reading and Language Arts Instruction	52	B	Social Studies Instruction
8	C	Reading and Language Arts Instruction	53	B	Social Studies Instruction
9	C	Reading and Language Arts Instruction	54	B	Social Studies Instruction
10	D	Reading and Language Arts Instruction	55	D	Social Studies Instruction
11	D	Reading and Language Arts Instruction	56	C	Social Studies Assessment
12	A	Reading and Language Arts Assessment	57	B	Social Studies Assessment
13	C	Reading and Language Arts Assessment	58	A	Social Studies Assessment
14	C	Reading and Language Arts Assessment	59	D	Social Studies Assessment
15	C	Reading and Language Arts Assessment	60	D	Arts and Physical Education Curriculum
16	B	Mathematics Curriculum	61	A	Arts and Physical Education Curriculum
17	C	Mathematics Curriculum	62	D	Arts and Physical Education Curriculum
18	D	Mathematics Curriculum	63	C	Arts and Physical Education Curriculum
19	D	Mathematics Curriculum	64	C	Arts and Physical Education Curriculum
20	D	Mathematics Instruction	65	B	Arts and Physical Education Curriculum
21	B	Mathematics Instruction	66	C	Arts and Physical Education Instruction
22	D	Mathematics Instruction	67	B	Arts and Physical Education Instruction
23	C	Mathematics Instruction	68	C	Arts and Physical Education Instruction
24	D	Mathematics Instruction	69	C	Arts and Physical Education Instruction
25	C	Mathematics Instruction	70	B	Arts and Physical Education Instruction
26	A	Mathematics Instruction	71	C	Arts and Physical Education Assessment
27	D	Mathematics Assessment	72	B	Arts and Physical Education Assessment
28	A	Mathematics Assessment	73	D	Arts and Physical Education Assessment
29	C	Mathematics Assessment	74	C	Arts and Physical Education
30	C	Mathematics Assessment	75	D	General Knowledge Curriculum
31	C	Science Curriculum	76	C	General Knowledge Curriculum
32	B	Science Curriculum	77	C	General Knowledge Curriculum
33	C	Science Curriculum	78	C	General Knowledge Curriculum
34	B	Science Curriculum	79	C	General Knowledge Curriculum
35	A	Science Instruction	80	A	General Knowledge Instruction
36	A	Science Instruction	81	D	General Knowledge Instruction
37	C	Science Instruction	82	B	General Knowledge Instruction
38	C	Science Instruction	83	B	General Knowledge Instruction
39	B	Science Instruction	84	C	General Knowledge Instruction
40	D	Science Instruction	85	B	General Knowledge Instruction
41	C	Science Instruction	86	B	General Knowledge Instruction
42	C	Science Assessment	87	C	General Knowledge Assessment
43	D	Science Assessment	88	A	General Knowledge Assessment
44	D	Science Assessment	89	B	General Knowledge Assessment
45	D	Social Studies Curriculum	90	B	General Knowledge Assessment

Explanations of Right Answers

1. In asking the students to "justify the Little Red Hen's decision," the teacher is helping the students to reason and make judgments and is encouraging them to develop and defend their decisions based on criteria they establish. "Evaluation" is the level of this task. Therefore, (D) is the correct answer.

2. Teachers are expected to understand the relationship of "parts" to "wholes" in the subject they teach and to apply this knowledge in designing learning activities. Although the activities listed in this question have a number of possible benefits for students as part of a language arts program, all are designed to expand readiness for reading. Because all are "prereading" activities, (B) is the correct answer.

3. This question asks about the language arts strategy least likely to be used by students during a social studies assignment. All of the possible strategies might be employed, but the question asks which "is LEAST likely to be used." Although memorization skills can be important, the assignment here is to write a short report, so long-term recall by commitment to memory is not the goal. Therefore, (D) is the correct answer.

4. Choices (B) and (D) may be appropriate for building interest in reading and enhancing reading readiness. (C) might be appropriate for practicing new skills. Only (A) combines teaching of the needed skills with meaningful contexts in which to use them. The correct answer, therefore, is (A).

5. During the publishing phase of the writing process, students make their writing public by reading, putting the writings in a booklet, and so on. The correct answer, therefore, is (D).

6. In the scenario presented here, the student has confused the word "son" (which is the desired word) with the word "sun," a word that sounds the same. Homophones are words that sound alike but have different meanings and spellings. Therefore, (D) is the correct answer.

7. Teachers must always be aware of the consequences of the learning activities they select. In this question, for example, the teacher might have chosen any one of these activities to follow up the reading of the novel. However, discussion in class about what students liked and disliked about the story is the most likely of the options to foster continued interest in the reading of fiction. Therefore, (B) is the correct answer.

8. This question asks about the skills that are most likely to be developed as a result of a specific activity. Another way to look at this question is to ask: "What is the goal of this assignment?" Identifying main ideas is the likely result of this activity. Newspaper headlines usually summarize the main ideas of the articles they describe. (C) is therefore the correct answer.

9. Analyzing student work can provide valuable insights into what a student can do and what additional work and activities are needed. A teacher needs to select developmentally appropriate strategies and adjust instructions accordingly to meet the needs of individual students. In this question, a first-grade student writes the words phonetically, as they are heard and not as they are spelled. Of all the options presented, "Explicit instruction in phonics and phonemic awareness" is most likely to assist the student in becoming a better speller. Therefore, (C) is the correct answer.

10. This question asks about oral book reports and the rationale for requiring students to present their reports orally. Note that it does not ask about other positive outcomes from oral presentations, but asks only which is the most likely motivator for reading. Oral book reports encourage students to share enjoyable reading experiences with others. This is a prime motivator both for the students who present reports and for the students who hear them. Therefore, (D) is the correct answer.

11. In addition to being able to use a variety of appropriate techniques in their teaching, teachers should be familiar with the theoretical bases of their approaches. This question asks you to demonstrate your knowledge of theory by presenting a teaching technique and inquiring about the theory that is being put into practice. (D) is the correct answer. Donald Holdaway and Marie Clay's work on literacy development shows the positive effects of keeping records of students' oral language and providing opportunities for shared, individualized, and guided reading.

12. Effective teaching depends on effective assessment. Teachers need to be able to assess their students' progress in order to plan assignments and classroom lessons. Standardized test results report the performance of students and groups of students who have taken the same test or tests. This is the kind of information this teacher needs. Therefore, (A) is the correct answer.

13. The question asks which of the four evaluative statements best assesses this student as a writer. Your task here is to read the sample and to evaluate it as if you were the teacher. (C) is the correct answer. The student's writing skills are adequately developed for the grade level.

14. There are many types of nontraditional assessments, including observation, oral reports, and running records. Here a fourth-grade teacher has students use portfolios for all their essays. The main value of student portfolios is for assessing the general development of skills and abilities over a period of time. Therefore, (C) is the correct answer.

15. Students make errors in their work that sometimes are random, but at other times they show a pattern or a common point of confusion shared among other students. This student has made some errors in pronoun usage, confusing subject pronouns (I, he, she, we, etc.) with objective ones (me, him, her, us, etc.). A review of proper usage of each type of pronoun as well as their word order placement (my Mom and I) would best help this student's writing. Therefore, (C) is the correct answer.

16. Mathematics teachers need to understand the skills that are required to perform mathematical tasks as well as the order in which their students can be expected to learn them. In this question, the most "concrete" task is one that involves physical manipulation, joining two blocks and four blocks (II). The next most abstract task is a graphic representation, adding apples shown in illustrations (III). Next is numeric, adding two numbers (I). The most abstract of the four tasks is solving for the unknown, here represented as x (IV). Therefore, (B) is the correct answer.

17. Arithmetic operations are an important part of elementary school mathematics. As in the previous question, you must understand the developmental hierarchy of skills students need to solve various kinds of problems. (C) is the correct answer. Dividing and multiplying fractions requires the most advanced understanding and the highest-order mathematical skills. It is a more complex task than (B) (adding fractions) or the tasks in (A) and (D) (adding whole numbers).

18. Teachers must be able to develop objectives that help their students meet overall curriculum goals. Here the goal is to use computational strategies accurately and to estimate appropriately. (D) is the correct answer because it covers both parts of the curricular goal. Students must understand the computational strategies involved in mathematics solutions before they are able to estimate or to evaluate estimated answers. None of the objectives reflected in the other options is as likely to meet the goal.

19. It is important for teachers to be familiar with all the various materials, technologies, and resources available to them. (D) is the correct answer. A geo-board would be least helpful to students copying line segments and angles onto paper. It is used to create figures like rectangles and triangles by stretching rubber bands over a board of evenly spaced nails. The other pieces of equipment are necessary for students to complete the assignment.

20. Real-life applications would not involve cut-out shapes, but common objects or situations. The teacher is helping to reinforce the angle definitions by asking the students to physically sort through the objects. The correct answer, therefore, is (D).

21. Here a teacher is assessing students' understanding by asking questions about measurement. The teacher has to be aware that students may know different systems for measuring length and weight; their correct answers may include feet, miles, meters, kilometers, pounds, and grams. The teacher has to be able to build on students' varied knowledge when teaching the unit. Therefore, (B) is the correct answer.

22. Here a teacher is "preteaching" students by having them use "mental mathematics" to compute simple multiplication problems before they tackle the actual problem that they will be asked to solve. Understanding the algorithm involved in multiplication is essential to success in solving multiplication problems. Using mental mathematics is a useful way to comprehend the algorithm. Therefore, (D) is the correct answer.

23. In this scenario, a teacher has students work in groups to come up with their own creative methods of solving a problem. The teacher is NOT encouraging the use of standard algorithms, but is encouraging the use of the other three strategies: estimation, guess and check, and cooperative learning. (C), therefore, is the correct answer.

24. Students have different learning styles and needs. Here you see four ways in which a teacher could respond to a student who does not understand the relationship between decimals and percents after it has been explained. The most appropriate response is to "reteach" the concept in new ways. In mathematics, it is useful to use different examples and to demonstrate, when possible, using manipulatives that students can see and touch. Therefore, (D) is the correct answer.

25. Teachers play a vital role in providing motivation for students. Practice is an important part of learning. Each of the four possible actions offered in the question deals with percentages, but the students are most likely to be motivated and achieve practice by the action described in (C). It involves them actively in applying what they know about percentages to a task that is likely to interest them: buying CDs at discount prices.

26. Teachers constantly translate theory into practice in the classroom. Their assignments are informed by what they have learned from the work of educational theorists. This teacher is using a "constructivist" approach with the class, letting the students "construct" their own answers. This allows the teacher both to see how her students are thinking and then to use these thought processes (and concrete examples) to introduce the concept of sets. Therefore, (A) is the correct answer.

27. Teachers are not only expected to understand how to use traditional and standardized testing methodologies, but they are also expected to be able to explain them to parents. Stanines divide a score scale into nine parts, with fixed percentages of students falling into each stanine. Dividing scores into stanines is a way of creating a "bell curve" and describing where a test taker's score falls within that bell-shaped curve. From stanines 1 to 5, the percentages are 4, 7, 12, 17, and 20, respectively. From stanines 6 to 9, the percentages are 17, 12, 7, and 4, respectively. Stanines 1, 2, and 3 are considered below average. Stanines 4, 5, and 6 are considered average, and stanines 7, 8, and 9 are considered above average. A score of 7 is somewhat above average. (D), therefore, is the correct answer.

28. A scale balance is a piece of equipment that needs to be used correctly in order to balance various materials. Students can best show that they have learned the necessary skill by individually "performing" in front of the teacher. The other strategies are not as appropriate because they do not include individual hands-on interaction with the balance. Thus, although the students might be able to describe the use of the balance, the teacher will not know whether they can actually use the equipment without seeing them use it. Therefore, (A) is the correct answer.

29. "The most common score" is the mode. "The arithmetic average" is the mean. "The highest score" is the maximum. A particular "median score" means that one-half of the students performed below that score and one-half performed above. (C), therefore, is the correct answer.

30. Patterns of errors can often reveal common points of confusion or misconception by students. In the examples given, the student does not understand that the fractions must be made to be equivalent before subtraction can take place. Instead, this student is subtracting numerators, then subtracting denominators, and putting one on top of the other to form the fraction that appears as the "answer." If this student applied the same approach to the problem $\frac{9}{11} - \frac{1}{7}$, the student would subtract 1 from 9 and 7 from 11, resulting in an answer of $\frac{8}{4}$. Therefore, (C) is the correct answer.

31. Presenting information graphically is a common goal of most science curriculums, and a useful teaching technique is to have students create their own graphs. In this question, students have produced both a table and a graph, but the results are in error because the students did not keep the intervals consistent on their vertical axis ("distance in meters"). Therefore, (C) is the correct answer. To facilitate their understanding, the teacher should explain (and demonstrate) how to use units of measure consistently on a graph.

32. Effective teachers are able to guide students from the specific findings of a "hands-on" experiment to the broader principles and theories behind the experimental results. The experiment described in the question exposes students to the odors of various familiar substances. The students observe the connection between the odor and the substance, plus the way odor is dispersed over distance. Since odor is a property of matter, this activity would fit into a science textbook under the heading "Physical Science: Properties of Matter." (B), therefore, is the correct answer.

33. Teachers must be able to understand, explain, and demonstrate how concepts can be utilized across disciplines. In the scenario presented here, the teacher is relating mathematics and science. Because students need to find the ratio between the mass of the cast iron and the distance that the spring is stretched, proportion is the key mathematical concept that the teacher is presenting. Therefore, (C) is the correct answer.

34. Teachers should be able to use a variety of curricular materials in their teaching. In the example given, it is most likely that the teacher has selected this book to stimulate students to use their imaginations in thinking about the sky. It is not likely that the teacher is providing facts for the students, nor is it likely that the teacher expects students of this age to understand the process of scientific inquiry. Therefore, (B) is the correct answer.

35. Teachers often need to identify and assess their students' acquisition of skills in a content area. In this example, having the individual student perform the required task is often the best way to identify and assess skills. It can be time-consuming, but it can also be the best method of assessment. (A), therefore, is the correct answer.

36. (A) is the correct answer. The teacher is varying instructional methods to meet the needs of all learners. By doing so, the teacher is increasing the opportunities for learning in the classroom.

37. Selecting appropriate teaching strategies is an important ingredient in a teacher's overall effectiveness in helping students learn. One of the primary goals of instruction is to keep students involved in their own education by having them be responsible as a group or as individuals for their learning. The teacher in the example uses the jigsaw method. Its premise is to break material down into smaller units, thereby allowing for more in-depth analysis, discussion, and teaching. Students will "assemble" the sections of the article into a whole as they are taught about each section by their fellow students. (C), therefore, is the correct answer.

38. Teachers should be able to adjust their instructional methods to meet the special needs of their students. Setting up an additional lab area in the classroom that is within reach of the student in a wheelchair is an effective course of action. Additionally, if the experiment is to be performed by groups of students, the physically challenged student should be included in a group, and all members of the group should work in the wheelchair-accessible lab area. Therefore, (C) is the correct answer.

39. Teachers must understand and be able to apply a variety of strategies for motivating students. "Extrinsic motivation" comes from *outside* the student. Offering rewards of any kind to students—whether they be tokens, stickers, candy, or a longer "recess" period—provides extrinsic motivation. (B), therefore, is the correct answer.

40. Teachers should be familiar with several methods of instruction, as well as the theories behind those methods, in order to adapt their teaching to meet a variety of learning styles present in a classroom of students. Graphic organizers, web diagrams, and illustrations all help visual learners, because they organize the material to be learned using a format that is easily accessible to these students. (D), therefore, is the correct answer.

41. When students assign rocks and minerals to groups according to key components and characteristics, they are classifying them. This is an important unifying concept in science instruction. (C), therefore, is the correct answer.

42. Key words in the question are "each student" and "explain." When you look at the possible answers, ask yourself which one offers the teacher the best opportunity to assess the level of understanding of *each student* in the class AND which offers individual students the best opportunity to *explain*. A true-or-false or multiple-choice test offers no opportunity for explanation. A small-group performance test does not allow the teacher to readily assess the skills of individual students, and the emphasis is on "doing" rather than "explaining." An essay test (also called a "constructed-response" test) offers the best opportunity for explaining the differences between mass and volume. (C), therefore, is the correct answer.

43. One of the more difficult tasks confronting teachers is deciding what to do if a significant number of students perform poorly on an assessment. Varying the methods and instructional materials is more likely to facilitate improved concept retention. Reteaching in this manner also represents reflective teaching. (D), therefore, is the correct answer.

44. When students investigate new concepts for themselves and construct their own explanations for what they have "discovered," they may not reach valid conclusions. Teachers have to be able to identify common points of confusion or misconception among their students and then develop new ways to reteach the material, while keeping students involved in their own learning and motivated to discover. In this question, you need to identify which of the options will be the LEAST likely to motivate students in pursuing learning. (D) is the correct answer. A teacher's goal should be to encourage students to actively discover answers for themselves and not to "get the right answer" from the teacher. Students are more likely to learn when they are actively involved. By providing "the answer," teachers are actually discouraging student involvement in their learning.

45. You should be familiar with the national standards in all of the fields you teach, in addition to knowing the requirements of your school or district curriculums. You also should be able to translate national curricular standards into classroom instruction. In the example given, asking why demand for oil increased with the invention of the automobile is a question that does implement the theme of "Time, Continuity, and Change." It asks students to analyze a historical event that has had profound consequences. This is clearly the only one of the four answer choices that offers this opportunity for analysis. (D), therefore, is the correct answer.

46. The correct sequencing of topics is essential in order for concepts and skills to build upon each other and for students to gain a deeper understanding of themes. The Articles of Confederation were the first constitution adopted by the thirteen colonies and went into effect in 1781. Because the individual colonies (and then states) retained so much power, the articles left the national government fairly weak. Because of this situation, many problems arose, including Shays' Rebellion, and the new Constitution was adopted with these defects in mind. Therefore, the Articles of Confederation are the best place to begin a unit on the United States Constitution. (B), therefore, is the correct answer. The other choices are all specific portions of the Constitution.

47. Social Studies students should be able to understand information and data that are represented visually—and they should be able to synthesize and present information and data themselves. The pie chart is an inappropriate choice for the task of showing changes over a period of time. Pie charts or circle graphs are good at showing relationships between the parts and the whole, and are therefore good for contrasting and comparing. Line graphs and bar graphs should be selected when students want to show changes over time. Therefore, (C) is the correct answer.

48. Teachers must always bear in mind whether their students are educationally and developmentally ready for the lessons they are planning. According to the table, reading a mileage chart is a graphic skill that is not taught until fourth grade. Therefore, third-grade students are not likely to have this skill. The teacher's planned activity is NOT appropriate for the grade level and the teacher's goal is NOT likely to be achieved. (D), therefore, is the correct answer.

49. "Assessment" is a continuum, from formal to informal. The example calls for an assessment technique that is not complicated or time-consuming. Although all of the techniques listed could be used as assessment techniques, only brainstorming meets the needs of the teacher for a simple but effective method of finding out what the students already know. (A), therefore, is the correct answer.

50. This question asks you to apply knowledge of basic economic principles to a real-life situation. The cold winter increases the demand for home heating oil at a time when the availability of oil (or "supply") does not proportionately increase. The price of the oil is likely to increase then because the demand increases and the supply does not. The correct answer is (C).

51. (A) is the correct answer. "Content integration" is the appropriate term for the activity presented in this scenario, where students use art to explore another culture as part of a social studies unit.

52. This is a question about teaching strategies. Although each of the possible activities might have merit as an activity, (B) is clearly the most effective way to teach this concept. It is the one that most actively involves students and it is the most personal, based on the actual experiences of students.

53. Teachers are required to adjust their methods of instruction constantly to meet the specific needs of their students. Of the options available, only (B) is an activity that engages students in critical thinking. They have to engage with the life situation of immigrants to be able to write about them.

54. Teachers have many strategies for motivating students, and teachers should know how to utilize age-appropriate strategies to encourage the success of their students. (B) is the correct answer. It is age-appropriate, it rewards students with an activity that is both fun and educational, and thus it is the most likely to motivate the entire class.

55. (D) is the correct answer. The assignment is too abstract for students of this age, who would not have a good concept of hemispheres. All the other activities are more appropriate for these students, since each one has a concrete task to encourage learning.

56. First, the teacher uses a "summative" assessment, assessing the "sum" of the objectives to see how well students have mastered them, and using this information to grade the students on their learning. Then, by comparing individual versus class performance statistics, the teacher is using "norm-referenced" assessment. Therefore, (C) is the correct answer.

57. A map is a form of "graphic representation." Social studies students are expected to be able to understand graphic representations of information, including data presented in maps, charts, and graphs. (B), therefore, is the correct answer.

58. Essay writing is frequently difficult for elementary-age students. Even though they may know the material well enough to answer multiple-choice or fill-in-the-blank questions, they often do poorly in essay questions. Essays require clarity of thought, adequate preparation, and direct writing that goes well beyond a surface understanding of the topic—and they require practice. A review, practice, and reassessment would be the most appropriate response. Therefore, (A) is the correct answer.

59. (D) names the only student whose list demonstrates an understanding of human "needs." All of the other lists represent "wants."

60. It is generally thought that elementary students do NOT have to be able to represent figures and objects with a high degree of accuracy. All of the other possible answers describe skills that are more important than accurate representation. Therefore, (D) is the correct answer.

61. When planning units of instruction, a teacher needs to be aware of the sequence as well as the content of the material. At times, lessons build on previous information or skills. At other times, lessons are developmentally appropriate for students only at a specific age. In this example, the teacher will most probably give instruction on team plays last, after basic individual skills have been developed. All the other answers represent individual skills and need to be developed before team play. (A), therefore, is the correct answer.

62. Fourth graders can certainly keep track of the distances they jump and can apply their mathematics skills to create a graph that shows the overall results of their jumps. (D), therefore, is the correct answer. The other examples either do not link math and physical education or are not developmentally appropriate.

63. A piano is a percussion instrument—felt-covered hammers hit strings to make sounds. All of the other choices do involve stringed instruments and are appropriate to use in this unit. (C), therefore, is the correct answer.

64. Music concepts should be prepared through various musical experiences prior to the formal presentation of the concept. Then the students should be given opportunities to use and practice this new knowledge. As students gain confidence and competence, opportunities to extend learning should be provided. The correct answer, therefore, is (C).

65. During aerobic exercise the body is using oxygen to produce the energy necessary to perform cardiorespiratory effort. The correct answer, therefore, is (B).

66. Brainstorming is most useful for teachers when it is most spontaneous. Students should be encouraged to contribute their ideas on a topic or answers to a question without "prescreening" their responses. This allows the teacher to see more accurately what the students know or believe. Statements (A), (B), and (D) all ask students to screen what they say before they say it. Only statement (C) accurately reflects the goal of brainstorming, and therefore it is the correct answer.

67. Using groups to create and demonstrate musical instruments is an example of cooperative learning—that is, learning activities in which students must work together to produce a result. (B), therefore, is the correct answer.

68. Knowing a broad range of teaching and learning strategies can benefit every teacher. Graphic organizers, webs, charts, etc., all help the visual learner, because information is organized in a display that makes it easier for these students to see relationships and understand concepts. (C), therefore, is the correct answer.

69. When a student is not learning the material that is being taught, the teacher must be able to find different ways of presenting the material until the student has demonstrated mastery. In this example, utilizing games that involve matching tones is the most likely of the four answer choices to assist the student in learning to sing on key. Therefore, (C) is the correct answer.

70. The teacher's strategy is an example of "positive reinforcement." The teacher is offering the students the opportunity to do something they like to do (play popular music) if they will first do something they do not like as much (play classical music). In other words, the students will receive a reward from the teacher (and will therefore be "positively reinforced" in their behavior). (B), therefore, is the correct answer.

71. Children in Piaget's concrete operational stage are able to take another's point of view and see more than one perspective simultaneously. They can understand concrete problems but not abstract ones, and they are not able to consider a range of logically possible outcomes for situations. Children who are not yet in this stage are not likely to be able to engage in a collective dialogue with their peers. (C), therefore, is the correct answer.

72. The key word here is "explain." An essay gives students an opportunity to explain what they know, to demonstrate a deeper understanding of the material, to show relationships between concepts, and to analyze the information through clear thinking and writing. This would be the best way to determine whether students understood the influences that were discussed in the unit on Romantic composers. (B), therefore, is the correct answer. The other choices are all appropriate methods of evaluation, but not for this particular material.

73. Portfolios generally contain students' work over a period of time. They allow the teacher and student either to see the progress made by the student or to see the best work by the student in a subject. In order to assess students' understanding of musical notes in the bass clef, a teacher might use a performance sample or a similar method that allows students to demonstrate their knowledge. (D), therefore, is the correct answer. The other answer choices are all better suited to assessment by the portfolio method.

74. With clear performance criteria in place for this physical activity, the teacher observation checklist is the most appropriate technique for evaluation. None of the other options is likely to yield useful results. Therefore, (C) is the correct answer.

75. The teacher is not using standardized tests to assess student understanding. Standardized tests are not always the best way to evaluate what students know, and effective teachers utilize a number of techniques to discover what their students understand and what they still need to learn. (D), therefore, is the correct answer.

76. (C) is the correct answer. By assigning an author, the teacher has taken away "choice," and this often leads to students being less enthusiastic about their reading. The other options include student choice and books that are "interesting and exciting."

77. (C) is the correct answer. Piaget's theories, based on observations of children, have implications for understanding how children think, how to use concrete materials in teaching, and how to sequence instruction. They do not have bearing on how to construct a rich social environment.

78. Both (A) and (D) treat the contributions of women as something out of the ordinary. (B) does not really provide an answer to the question. (C) is the correct answer.

79. This question asks you to apply your knowledge of interactions with parents. Parents or guardians should be given regular opportunities to meet with the teacher at the school so that they can express particular needs and raise questions, even if in limited English. The other options may be desirable in some ways, but are not practical. The correct answer, therefore, is (C).

80. A "concept map" is a visual web or diagram of how concepts are related to each other. It is most useful as an instrument to assess students' understanding of major concepts or themes and can be used appropriately by teachers before teaching a new unit (to see what students already know) or at the end of a unit (to see what students have learned and what they have not yet mastered). However, it is not useful for assessing students' progress when they are writing reports. (A), therefore, is the correct answer.

81. All of the proposed activities are appropriate ways to accommodate difference except for focusing classroom discussions on a particular group of minority students. Therefore, (D) is the correct answer.

82. Integrating the teaching of the curriculum is a goal for all elementary school teachers. Here a teacher is using a novel to discuss topics in social studies. This is an example of "integration through thematic units." (B), therefore, is the correct answer.

83. In "cooperative learning," students generally work together as a team, and the group's work as a whole is graded or evaluated. This approach generates many positive outcomes, several of which are addressed in this question. However, development of time management skills is not a primary goal of this kind of instruction. (B), therefore, is the correct answer.

84. Some students are not able to work well in cooperative groups and their behavior may affect the overall productivity of the group. In the example, allowing the student to participate in the group is essential for the growth and development of the student, but this student will also benefit from individual work with the teacher—and so will the group. (C), therefore, is the correct answer.

85. "Wait time" is often "thinking time." It allows students to comprehend a teacher's question and come up with an answer. (B), therefore, is the correct answer. Other strategies are more effective when students are not focused, are embarrassed, or are already speaking.

86. Kinesthetic learners are most likely to learn from acting out the concepts being taught. Discussing, writing, and reading are approaches that are not likely to be as successful with kinesthetic learners. Therefore, (B) is the correct answer.

87. (C) is the correct answer. "Criterion referenced" refers to a test in which the correct answers are calculated, by category, against objectives.

88. A "working" portfolio is generally considered to be the most accurate because it contains all of the student's work to date in a specific subject. It allows both the teacher and the student to see the progress that has been made and to identify areas in which the student still needs to develop. (A), therefore, is the correct answer. A "showcase" portfolio usually contains a student's best work in a subject. A "record-keeping" portfolio usually refers to a portfolio kept by the teacher for each student, with contents such as notes from the student's parents and anecdotal records taken by the teacher based on observing the student. A "teacher" portfolio usually describes a portfolio kept by the teacher that includes assignments given to the class, along with data on student performance and notes about the success of each assignment.

89. (B) is the correct answer. Norm-referenced tests are judged in comparison with standards determined by testing a selected group of people: the standardized sample.

90. By focusing on the meaning of an unfamiliar word as it relates to the rest of the paragraph, the teacher is highlighting the use of context clues. (B), therefore, is the correct answer.

Chapter 7
Are You Ready? Last-Minute Tips

▶   ▶   ▶   ▶   ▶   ▶   ▶   ▶   ▶   ▶   ▶   ▶

Checklist

Complete this checklist to determine whether you're ready to take the test.

❏ Do you know the testing requirements for your field in the state(s) where you plan to teach?

❏ Have you followed all of the test registration procedures?

❏ Do you know the topics that will be covered in each test you plan to take?

❏ Have you reviewed any textbooks, class notes, and course readings that relate to the topics covered?

❏ Do you know how long the test will take and the number of questions it contains? Have you considered how you will pace your work?

❏ Are you familiar with the test directions and the types of questions on the test?

❏ Are you familiar with the recommended test-taking strategies and tips?

❏ Have you worked through the practice test questions at a pace similar to that of an actual test?

❏ If you are repeating a Praxis Series™ Assessment, have you analyzed your previous score report to determine areas where additional study and test preparation could be useful?

The Day of the Test

You should end your review a day or two before the actual test date. The day of the test you should

- Be well rested

- Take photo identification with you

- Take a supply of well-sharpened #2 pencils (at least three)

- Take your admission ticket, letter of authorization, mailgram, or telegram with you

- Eat before you take the test to keep your energy level up

- Wear layered clothing; room temperature may vary

- Be prepared to stand in line to check in or to wait while other test takers are being checked in

You can't control the testing situation, but you can control yourself. Stay calm. The supervisors are well trained and make every effort to provide uniform testing conditions, but don't let it bother you if the test doesn't start exactly on time. You will have the full amount of time once it does start.

Think of preparing for this test as training for an athletic event. Once you've trained, prepared, and rested, give it everything you've got. Good luck.

Appendix A
Study Plan Sheet

▶ ▶ ▶ ▶ ▶ ▶ ▶ ▶ ▶ ▶ ▶ ▶

Study Plan Sheet

See chapter 1 for suggestions on using this Study Plan Sheet.

STUDY PLAN						
Content covered on test	How well do I know the content?	What material do I have for studying this content?	What material do I need for studying this content?	Where could I find the materials I need?	Dates planned for study of content	Dates completed

Appendix B
For More Information

▶   ▶   ▶   ▶   ▶   ▶   ▶   ▶   ▶   ▶   ▶   ▶

ETS offers additional information to assist you in preparing for the Praxis Series™ Assessments. *Tests at a Glance* materials and the *Registration Bulletin* are both available without charge (see below to order). You can also obtain more information from our Web site: www.ets.org/praxis.

General Inquiries

Phone: 800-772-9476 or 609-771-7395, (Monday–Friday, 8:00 a.m. to 7:45 p.m., Eastern time)
Fax: 609-771-7906

Extended Time

If you have a learning disability or if English is not your primary language, you can apply to be given more time to take your test. The *Registration Bulletin* tells you how you can qualify for extended time.

Disability Services

Phone: 866-387-8602 or 609-771-7780
Fax: 609-771-7906
TTY (for deaf or hard-of-hearing callers): 609-771-7714

Mailing Address

ETS–The Praxis Series™
P.O. Box 6051
Princeton, NJ 08541-6051

Overnight Delivery Address

ETS–The Praxis Series™
Distribution Center
225 Phillips Blvd.
P.O. Box 77435
Ewing, NJ 08628-7435